Entering the Biblical Text
Exploring Jewish Values in the Torah

Entering the Biblical Text
Exploring Jewish Values in the Torah

Ronald H. Isaacs

Ktav Publishing House, Inc.

Library of Congress Cataloging-in-Publication Data

Isaacs, Ronald H.
    Entering the biblical text: exploring Jewish values in the Torah / Ronald H. Isaacs.
    p. cm.
Includes bibliographical references.
ISBN 0-88125-699-4
    1. Bible. O.T. Pentateuch--Criticism, interpretation, etc. 2. Ethics in the Bible. 3. Justice--Biblical teaching. 4. Obedience-- Biblical teaching. 5. Trust in God--Biblical teaching. I. Title.

BS1225.3 .I82 2000
222'.106--dc21

00-046500

Distributed by
Ktav Publishing House, Inc.
900 Jefferson Street
Hoboken, NJ 07030
201-963-9524 FAX 201-963-0102
Email ktav@compuserve.com

Contents

Introduction

The Bible is the oldest and most widely read book in our civilization. It has been in continuous circulation for almost two thousand years and has been the source of religious ideals and values for millions of people. Ever since Sinai, the moral imperatives of the Torah—the Five Books of Moses and the books of the Prophets have provided great inspiration to social reformers and religious idealists.

Throughout the English-speaking world many famous writers, poets and dramatists have studied the Bible for its profound issues and values. Political ideas and institutions have been shaped by biblical teachings.

The first five books of the Bible comprise the Torah, and are regarded as Judaism's central document. Along with the stories about the patriarchs Abraham, Isaac and Jacob, the matriarchs Sarah, Rebekah, Rachel and Leah, and Moses and the exodus of the Israelites from Egypt, they contain the 613 commandments, the backbone of all of later Jewish law. Indeed our values in almost every area of life are suffused with images and concepts from the Bible.

The goal of this book is to provide students with an entry into the Bible that will help them to explore important contemporary issues and problems that are manifested in twelve important and challenging Bible stories in the Torah.

Each chapter will be divided into the following sections:

The Bible Story: This will present the narrative of the story, directly from the Bible.

The Problem: This will identify the theme and the problems and questions that are raised by the story.

What the Commentaries Say: This will present various commentaries as culled from both ancient rabbinic and modern sources. (Note: When a particular commentary revolves around a key verse, the verse will be included for quick reference.)

Questions: This will present questions to answer. Students are encouraged to re-read the Bible story, and use the commentaries as guidelines when trying to answer the questions.

The stories have been selected because of the variety of issues that they bring to bear. They are stimulating, challenging and intriguing tales that are certain to delight the reader. Answering the questions and doing the exercises should enable the reader to acquire a deeper understanding of the biblical story and a richer appreciation of its message.

I. Abraham's Plea for Sodom

Should good people suffer for the evil of bad people?

The Bible Story (Genesis 18:20–33)

20. Then God said: "The outrage of Sodom and Gomorrah is great, and their sin is so severe. 21. I will go down to see whether they have acted altogether according to the outcry that has come to Me; if not, I will take note.

22. The men went on from there to Sodom, while Abraham remained standing before God. 23. Abraham came forward and said,"Will You take away the innocent along with the guilty?" 24. What if there should be fifty innocent people within the city. Will You still wipe out and not forgive it for the sake of the innocent fifty who are in it? 25. Far be it from You to do such a thing, to bring death on the innocent as well as on the guilty, so that the guilty and innocent are treated alike. Far be it from You. Shall not the Judge of all the earth act with justice?" 26. And God answered,"If I find within the city of Sodom fifty innocent ones, I will forgive the entire place for their sake."

27. Abraham spoke up saying, "Here I attempt to speak to God, I who am but dust and ashes. 28.What if the

fifty innocent should lack five? Will You still destroy the whole city for want of the five?" And God answered: "I will not destroy it if I find forty-five there." 29. But he spoke to God again, and said: "What if forty should be found there?" And God answered: "I will not do it for the sake of the forty." 30. And he said, "Let not God be angry if I go on: What if thirty shall be found there?" And God answered,"I will not do it if I find thirty there."

31. And he said, "I attempt again to speak to my God: What if I find twenty there?" And God answered,"I will not destroy for the sake of twenty." 32. And he said: "Let not God be angry if I speak but this last time: What if ten should be found there?" And God answered, "I will not destroy for the sake of the ten."

33. When God had finished speaking to Abraham, God departed. And Abraham returned to his place.

The Problem

The town of Sodom has become today a byword for self-ishness and cruelty. Despite both Sodom and twin-city Gomorrah's reputation for cruelty, when God shares with Abraham His intention to destroy the cities, Abraham tries to change God's mind. He asks: Since there are undoubtedly some good people in the cities, how can God destroy the innocent with the wicked: "Shall not the Judge of all the earth act with justice?" (Genesis 18:25) One of the problems in this story is that Abraham also seems to be arguing on behalf of the evil people. Otherwise, he would have requested that the good people alone be spared. Instead, Abraham appeals to God to save all the people of Sodom and Gomorrah, provided some good people be found within them.

This is the first instance recorded in the Torah of a human being arguing with God. Does Abraham really doubt the existence of God's justice? Is it permissible to "bargain" and argue with God? We see in the story that God does not reject Abraham's question about His justice. It is possible to argue with God, but God, it appears, always has the last word.

What the Commentaries Say

Be'er Mayim Chayim: "Will you punish the innocent along with the wicked?" (Genesis 18:23) The rule is that when the good predominate in the world and good deeds exceed the bad, the wicked, too, are saved through the merits of the righteous. The reverse, though, that when the wicked predominate the good should be punished alongside the wicked, is not true, for that would be unjust. As to the variance between the two cases, our Sages tell us that God's attributes of doing good exceeds His attribute of punishing people five hundred times over, namely that if a good deed and an evil deed are of equal rank, the reward for the good deed will be five hundred times the punishment for the evil deed.

Nahum Sarna: "Shall not the Judge of all the earth act with justice?" (Genesis 18:25) The Bible is concerned with the problem of divine justice. Just because God is universal and omnipotent, mankind needs assurance that God's mighty power is not indiscriminately employed and that God's ways are not capricious. God must act according to a principle that man can try to understand, and that principle is the passion for righteousness. Thus, when Abraham asks the questions, "Will you sweep away the innocent along with the guilty? Shall not the Judge of all the earth act justly," it is taken for granted that the respective answers cannot possibly be other than a resounding, "Of course not." "Absolutely."

Tosefta: Because of their wealth, the people of Sodom became haughty. They said to one another: "Since gold and silver flow from our land, why should we allow strangers to visit in our borders, eat our food, use our resources, and share what is ours? They will only take what we have, and there will be less for us. Let's keep them from entering, and let's drive out those who get in as soon as possible—especially the poor or the sick ones."

Gunther Plaut: "I will not destroy for the sake of ten." (Genesis 25:32) Abraham does not plead merely for the innocent but for the sinners as well, through the merit of the righteous (*zechut avot*). The story of Sodom and Gomorrah introduces the concept of merit, which stipulates that a handful of concerned, decent and righteous people could have averted Sodom's calamity by their merit. The story also suggests that there are limits to the influence of even the best people. Unless they find a minimum of like-minded associates, they will be ineffective. Eventually, if they persist in living in such a society, they will perish with it. Thus, Abraham, in his pursuit of divine equity, does not go below the number ten.

Arnold Zweig: When Abraham could not find fifty righteous men in Sodom, and pleaded on behalf of forty, thirty, twenty, ten, that the great city might be spared, do you think that God did not know all the time that there were not even ten righteous men in Sodom? But God wanted our father, Abraham to show whether he was a man or not. And didn't he show himself a man.

Midrash Genesis Rabbah 49:6: "I will go down to see whether they have acted according to the outcry that has come to Me." (Genesis 18:21) Why did God say "I will go down to see"? God wanted to give the cities time to repent. This teaches that a judge must carefully examine a case before pronouncing judgment, and further, that just as God "went down" to see, so must man not judge his fellow man until he has come to see things from the other's viewpoint.

Questions

1. Why does God say: "I will go down to see whether they have acted according to the outcry that has reached Me; if not, I will take note?"

2. There is one theme, namely that of repentance, which is strangely absent from this story. Neither Abraham nor the

messengers warn the people of Sodom of the impending disaster in the hope of arousing them to atonement. Why do you think this is so?

3. Abraham in this story questions God. What are some times when you have questioned God? Do you think it is appropriate to question God?

4. Why does Abraham not go below the number ten in his attempt to find ten righteous people? Was Abraham able to change God's mind?

5. On whose behalf did Abraham intercede? To save only the righteous, or the wicked as well?

6. At the end of the story, the Bible tells us that "Abraham returned to his place?" What do you think that this means?

7. What was the sin of the Sodomites? Why did it make God so angry that God decided to destroy the entire city?

8. What is the moral of this Bible story? Can you think of a contemporary situation where a person confronts the justice system?

II. The Sacrifice of Isaac
What is true loyalty to God?

The Bible Story (Genesis 22:1–19)

1. Some time later, God put Abraham to the test. God said to him: "Abraham," and he answered, "Here I am." 2. And God said: "Take your son, your favorite one, Isaac, the one whom you love and proceed to the land of Moriah, and offer him on one of the high places that I will show you." 3. So early the next morning Abraham saddled his donkey and took with him his two servants and his son Isaac. He split the wood for the burnt offering, and he set out for the place which God had told him. 4. On the third day Abraham looked up and saw that place in the distance. 5. Then Abraham said to his servants,"You stay here with the donkey. The boy and I will go up there, and we will worship and return to you."

6. Abraham took the wood for the burnt offering and put it on his son Isaac. He took the firestone and the knife, and the two of them walked off together. 7. Then Isaac said to his father Abraham: "Father." And he answered, "Yes my son."

And he said: "Here are the firestone and the wood, but where is the sheep for the burnt offering?" 8. And Abraham said: "God will provide the sheep for the burnt offering, my son. And the two of them walked together.

9. They arrived at the place which God told him. There Abraham built an altar. He laid out the wood and bound his son Isaac. He laid him on the altar, on top of the wood. 10. Abraham picked up the knife to slay his son. 11. Then an angel of God called to him from heaven: "Abraham, Abraham." And he answered, "Here I am." 12. And he said: "Do not raise your hand against the boy, or do anything to harm him. For now I know that you fear God, since you have not withheld your son, your favored one, from Me." 13. When Abraham looked up, his eye glanced upon a ram, caught in the bushes by its horn. So Abraham went and took the ram and offered it up as a burnt offering in place of his son. 14. And Abraham named that site Adonai-yireh, whence the present saying, "On the mount of God there is vision."

15. The angel of God called to Abraham a second time from heaven, 16. and said, "By Myself I swear, God declares: Because you have done this and have not withheld your son, your favored one, 17. I will bestow My blessing upon you and make your descendants as plentiful as the stars of heaven and sands of the seashore, and your descendants shall seize the gates of their foes. 18. All the nations of the earth shall bless themselves by your descendants, because you have obeyed My command." 19. So Abraham returned to his servants, and they departed together for Beer-sheba, and Abraham stayed in Beer-sheba.

The Problem

The story of Abraham being called by God to sacrifice his beloved son Isaac is a most frightening one. It was also considered one of the most important events in the entire Torah. The rabbis titled the story *Akedat Yitzchak*, "the binding of Isaac for a sacrifice" and chose it for reading on Rosh Hashanah. They believed that it was a "test" for Abraham's loyalty to God. The test of Abraham is perhaps the most difficult test of faith, trust and loyalty to God that could be devised. It is an ultimate test, in that it asks Abraham to give up his beloved son.

In the traditional understanding of the story, God never intended for Abraham to slaughter Isaac, because it was wrong—as we know from the end of the story when Abraham is told to put down his knife. Abraham, on the other hand, out of loyalty to God, was willing to violate God's moral law against murder to which Abraham was committed.

One of the central problems that readers of the Bible have with Abraham's behavior is that he so easily acquiesces to God's command to kill his son Isaac. He seems to do so without hesitation, without asking any questions, with even consulting his wife Sarah. And thus, one of the major questions of this story is: How ought a person to show his or her loyalty to God? Should a person who hears God's voice asking him/her to do something contrary to moral law do it without question? What kind of a God would ask a person to sacrifice his beloved son?

What the Commentaries Say

Following is a cross-section of commentary (both rabbinic and modern) related to the story. Read each of the commentaries and discuss which ones with which you are most likely to agree or disagree.

1. **Moses Maimonides**: "For now I know that you fear God, since you have not withheld your favorite son from Me." (Genesis 22:12)

The purpose of all tests in the Torah is to teach people how they are to act. Abraham is commanded to sacrifice his son Isaac. And because he feared God and loved to do whatever God commanded, he thought little of his beloved child, and set aside all his hopes concerning him, and agreed to kill him. Therefore, the angel said to him: "For now I know that you fear God," which means that from Abraham's action, we can learn how far we must go in the fear of God.

2. **Abarbanel**: The story of Abraham's faith is an example, a banner for all the peoples of the world to follow. Loyalty to God does not mean "blind faith." Sometimes it means asking difficult questions about what it is that we should or should not do. Sometimes it means being prepared to take risks for what we believe is just and right. The *Akedah* story is a story about Abraham's struggle to understand what it means to be loyal to God. He is an example of a person who tested his faith with questions and weighed his decisions carefully. If necessary, he was prepared to make sacrifices for what he

believed, but he was also ready to rethink his convictions and commitments. Thus the story of Abraham is considered one of the great examples of religious faith and loyalty to God.

3. **Reb Menachem Mendl of Kotzk:** "On the third day Abraham looked and saw the place from afar." (Genesis 22:4) The Torah states that "on the third day Abraham lifted up his eyes, and saw the place from afar." (Genesis 22:4) Abraham's greatness in the sacrifice was that even on the third day he was as enthusiastic as he had been on the first. Momentary fervor is not that great a test. But on the third day, after a long and difficult journey, Abraham was still as enthusiastic as he had been at the beginning, and was able to lift up his eyes with the same intensity.

4. **Lippman Bodoff:** In the story of the *Akedah* God was testing Abraham to see if he would remain loyal to God's moral law, but Abraham, who could not know this, was simultaneously testing God to see what kind of covenant and religion he, Abraham, was being asked to join. In testing God, as it were, Abraham was ultimately testing himself. Abraham wanted to see if God would stop him, so Abraham used the strategy of stalling for time. I do not believe that Abraham ever intended to kill Isaac. Rather, by not rushing and taking his time, Abraham tried to give God time to change His mind. Abraham never agrees to accept God's command and perform it. Instead, Abraham goes through a series of separate steps: First he gets up, then he dresses his

animals, then he gets his retinue in order, then he cuts firewood, and then he sets off, and then he sees Moriah, and
then he instructs his servants to wait, and then he takes the
firewood, and then he takes the fire and the knife. At each
step of the way Abraham is waiting for God to withdraw His
command. When that is not forthcoming, Abraham takes the
next step and puts God to the next test—as it were—always
showing obedience and always giving God the chance to
make the moral statement that God does not want man to
murder in God's name.

5. **Dvora Yanow**: Professor Yanow relates a commentary
written by the sister of the great biblical commentator Rashi.
The commentary asks where Sarah is while the story of her
husband Abraham and son Isaac takes place. Sarah's voice is
nowhere to be heard. Some have suggested that Sarah is not
present in the Bible story because Abraham did not tell her of
his plans. Others have suggested that Abraham did tell her
and that this is precisely why she is silent: Sarah is in a state
of shock over Abraham's intentions. Some see this shock as
the reason for Sarah's death at the beginning of the subse-
quent chapter (Genesis 23:2).

Professor Yanow proposes that the reason that Sarah is
silent in the sacrifice story is because the events are unfold-
ing in a dream in a delayed reaction to Isaac's circumcision,
a dream spawned perhaps by drinking too much at the
drinking feast that Abraham made on the day of Isaac's
weaning (Genesis 21:8). Sarah doesn't speak because in her
dream she is working out her emotional reactions to the cir-

cumcision. Thus the knife in the story that Abraham takes with him is not for the sacrifice of his son, but rather for his circumcision!

Professor Jeffrey H. Tigay: "Take your son, your only son, whom you love, Isaac. (Genesis 22:2) If we want to understand the *Akedah*, we must try to understand what God's command would have meant to a person living in Abraham's time. Perhaps the clue to God's purpose is in the wording of God's command: "Take your son, your only one, whom you love, Isaac, and go forth to the land of Moriah and offer him there as a burnt offering on one of the heights that I will show you." The style of God's command, the words "go forth," the listing of what is being given up, the vagueness of the destination—recalls God's words to Abraham years earlier: "Go forth from your land and your kindred and your father's house to the land that I will show you." It is in this stylistic similarity that we find the meaning of the *Akedah*. When God first called Abraham to follow him, Abraham and Sarah were respectively, 75 and 65 years old and childless. Yet God promised Abraham a nation full of descendants. Abraham followed and God gave him Ishmael and Isaac. After Ishmael was sent away, it was only through Isaac that God's promise could be fulfilled. In the *Akedah*, by subtly reminding Abraham of God's original promise while asking him to forgo that promise by sacrificing the son through whom it would be realized, God tested whether Abraham's devotion was based on expected reward or was unconditional.

Questions

1. If you were Abraham and did not know what God truly had in mind in terms of the ultimate sacrifice of your son, would you have acted in a similar fashion? Is this the kind of loyalty that God demands of each and every one of us?

2. Is the story of the sacrifice of Isaac what true faith is all about?

3. Are there things that you would have expected Abraham to do that he did not do? If so, what are they?

4. Do you think that Abraham would have really gone through with the sacrifice of his son if the angels had not stopped him? Prove it from the text.

5. Why is Abraham so silent in the story? Compare this story to the previous story of Sodom and Gomorrah in Genesis 18: 22–33. Which Abraham do you prefer in terms of his actions in each story? Why?

6. What is the purpose of the servants in the story? Why do you think that Abraham takes them along with him, and why does he leave them by themselves along the way?

7. Why do you think that God uses angels rather than His own voice in order to stop Abraham from killing his son?

Why does God need to use two angels?

8. How old do you think Isaac was in this story? Prove it from the text? Do you think that Isaac knew what was about to happen to him?

9. Can you find any significant words in this story that tend to be "repeaters"? What are the words, and why do you think they are used with such frequency?

10. Why do you think that some Christians believe that this story is a paradigm of Jesus as a sacrificial lamb? Give several proofs if possible.

11. According to some rabbinic interpreters, Abraham had questions and doubts about what God had commanded him to do. Look at the story carefully, and see whether you can find examples of Abraham's doubts by virtue of his actions in the story. Did Abraham act recklessly and impetuously throughout the story? Or do you perceive that Abraham (because he had his doubts) used "stall" tactics in order to bide time and try to figure out what God really had in mind.

12. Why does Abraham have to sacrifice a ram?

13. What is strange about the way in which the story ends?

14. Are we to follow the commandments of our faith without questioning them? Are we disloyal if we express doubts about what Jewish tradition says God "commands" us to do?

15. What do you think is the ultimate purpose of Abraham's test?

16. Since many people in Abraham's time believed in child sacrifice, perhaps the true message of the story is that God does not desire human sacrifice. If this be so, then what are some ways in which modern society "sacrifices" children? How can children be protected from being victimized by the many bad elements of the culture that surrounds us?

III. The Blessing of Jacob and Esau

Under what circumstances are cheating and lying permitted?

The Bible Story (Genesis 25:22–23, 29–33; 27:1–40)

Chapter 25

22. Rebekah went to inquire of God, 23. and God answered her:

"Two nations are in your womb. . . . One people shall be mightier than the other, and the older shall serve the younger."

29. Once, when Jacob was cooking stew, Esau came in from the open, famished. 30. Esau said to Jacob, "Give me some of that red soup to eat, for I am starving." . . . 31. Jacob said: "First sell me your birthright." 32. Esau answered: "I am at the point of death, so of what use is the birthright to me?"

33. But Jacob said, "Swear to me first." So he swore to him and sold his birthright to Jacob. 34. Then Jacob gave Esau bread and stew, and he ate and drank and rose and went away. Thus did Esau spurn the birthright.

Chapter 27

1. When Isaac was old and his eyes were too dim to see, he called his older son Esau and said to him: "My son." Esau answered: "Here I am." 2. And he said: "I am elderly, and I do not know how soon I may die. 3. Take your gear, your quiver and bow, and go out into the open and hunt some game for me. 4. Then prepare a rich dish for me that I enjoy, and bring it to me to eat, that I may give you my innermost blessing before I die.

5. Rebekah had been listening as Isaac spoke to his son Esau. When Esau had gone out into the open to hunt game to bring home, 6. Rebekah said to her son Jacob: "I overheard your father speaking to your brother Esau, saying, 7. 'Bring me some game and prepare a dish for me to eat, that I may bless you, with God's approval before I die.' 8. My son, listen carefully to my instructions. 9. Go to the flock and bring me two choice kids, and I will make a dish for your father such as he loves. 10. Then take it to your father to eat, in order that he may bless you before he dies." 11. Jacob answered his mother Rebekah: "But my brother Esau is a hairy man and I am smooth-skinned. 12. If my father touches me, I shall appear to him as a deceiver and bring upon myself a curse, not a blessing." 13. But his mother said to him, "Your curse, my son, will be upon me. Just do as I say and go fetch them to me." 14. He got them and brought them to his mother, and his mother prepared a dish such as his father liked. 15. Rebekah then took the best clothes of her older son Esau, which were in the house, and had her younger son Jacob put

them on. 16. She covered his hands and the hairless part of his neck with the skins of the kids. 17. Then she placed in the hands of her son Jacob the dish and the bread that she had prepared.

18. He went to his father and said, "Father." And he said, "Yes, which of my sons are you?" 19. Jacob said to his father, "I am Esau, your first-born. I have done what you told me to do. Please sit up and eat of my game, that you may give me your innermost blessing." 20. Isaac then said to his son, "How did you succeed so quickly, my son?" And he said, "Because God granted me good fortune." 21. Isaac then said to Jacob, "Come closer that I may feel you, my son—whether you are really my son Esau or not." 22. So Jacob drew close to his father Isaac, who touched him and wondered, "The voice is the voice of Jacob, and yet the hands are the hands of Esau." 23. He did not recognize him, because his hands were hairy like those of his brother Esau. And so he blessed him.

24. He then asked, "Are you really my son Esau?" 25. And when he said, "I am," he said, "Serve me and let me eat of my son's game that I may give you my most innermost blessing." So he served him and he ate, and he brought him wine and he drank. 26. Then his father Isaac said to him, "Come close and kiss me, my son." 27. And he went up and kissed him. And he smelled his clothes and blessed him, saying, "The smell of my son is like the smell of the fields that God has blessed. Let peoples serve you, and nations bow to you."

30. No sooner had Jacob left his father's presence, after

Isaac had finished blessing Jacob, than his brother Esau came back from the hunt. 31. He too prepared a dish and brought it to his father. And he said to his father, "Let my father sit up and eat of his son's game, so that you may give me your innermost blessing." 32. His father Isaac then said to him, "Who are you?" And he said, "I am your son Esau, your first-born." 33. Isaac trembled greatly and violently. "Who was it then," he demanded, "that hunted game and brought it to me? Moreover, I ate of it before you came, and I blessed him. Now he must remain blessed." 34. When Esau heard his father's words, he uttered a great and exceedingly bitter cry and said to his father, "Bless me too, father." 35. But he answered: "Your brother came with shrewdness and took away your blessing." 36. Esau then said, "Was he then named Jacob that he might supplant me these two times? First he took my birthright and now he has taken away my blessing." And he added: "Have you not reserved a blessing for me?"

37. Isaac answered, saying to Esau: "But I have made him master over you. I have given him all his brothers for ser-vants, and sustained him with grain and wine. What then, can I still do for you, my son?" 38. And Esau said to his father, "Have you then but one blessing, my father?" Bless me too, father." And Esau cried aloud. 39. And his father answered, saying to him, "Behold, your dwelling shall be the fatness of the earth and the dew of heaven above. 40. By your sword you shall live, and you shall serve your brother."

The Problem

For a short time after their marriage, Isaac and Rebekah have difficulty conceiving. Finally, she becomes pregnant. Soon thereafter she learns from none other than God that she is carrying twins and that from them, two battling nations will emerge. When the children are born, the eldest twin is called Esau (meaning "hairy") and the younger child named Jacob (meaning "heel") because at birth his hand was holding onto Esau's heel. As they grow Esau becomes a skilled hunter while Jacob quietly remains within the camp. Isaac continually favors Esau because he brings him food that he enjoys, while mother Rebekah favors Jacob.

In the Bible story which you will now study, Esau, who one day finds himself extremely hungry, sells his birthright to Jacob in exchange for some stew. Later, near the time of father Isaac's death, Isaac asks Esau to go out hunting and bring him a tasty dish, promising that he will reward Esau with a special blessing. Rebekah overhears their conversation and persuades Jacob to dress in Esau's clothing and to put on hairy skins so that he will fool Isaac into believing that he is Esau. His disguise does apparently fool his father, and Isaac, believing that he is blessing Esau, blesses him with the words "Let peoples serve you, and nations bow to you." When Esau returns from the field with a tasty dish, as his father had requested, Isaac informs him that he has already given away his blessing. Esau is outraged and angry, even threatening to kill his brother Jacob. The story concludes with Isaac blessing Esau with the words: "Your abode shall enjoy the fat of the earth, and the dew of heaven above, and by your sword shall you live."

This story is bound to leave the reader with the absence of moral judgment. Jacob, with his mother's help, practices outrageous deceit on his helpless father and a guileless brother, and he is rewarded for his deed. Does the Torah condone trickery and deception? Are there times when not telling the truth and deceiving are permissible in Judaism?

There is another serious problem in connection with the upbringing of Jacob and Esau. We are told in the Torah that Isaac loved Esau, whereas Rebekah loved Jacob. How is it possible that there would be favoritism in the household of a man and a woman who have today become one of the patriarchs and matriarchs of Judaism?

What the Commentaries Say

Adin Steinsaltz: He posits that Rebekah had grown up in the "wheeling and dealing" corrupt world of her brother Laban, learning the meaning of cheating and hypocrisy. She was a realist where Isaac was an easy victim of duplicity. He was neither suspicious nor afraid because there was no dishonesty in his own heart. For those reasons, Isaac did not notice Esau's weaknesses but only that he seemed well-behaved and did what his father requested of him. On the other hand, Rebekah was an expert in such matters. She knew that someone like Esau could have another, less pleasant aspect, an aspect that reminded her of her brother Laban. She recognized her own family in Esau, and she knew his

shortcomings and his weak points. As a result of this understanding, she manipulated Isaac into blessing Jacob instead
of Esau out of her love for Isaac, in an attempt to shield and
protect him from the emotional shock of his own error.
(**Note:** In other words, Rebekah favored Jacob not only
because she knew that Esau possessed shortcomings like her
brother Laban, but also because she wished to protect her
husband Isaac from making a mistake by giving Esau and
not Jacob his blessing. Thus Rebekah's favoritism was a form
of saving Isaac from his own foolish decisions.)

Midrash HaGadol: "Two nations are in your womb . . .
and the older shall serve the younger." (Genesis 25:23)
Rebekah showed partiality toward Jacob because she, more
than Isaac or anyone else, had a mother's intuition that Jacob
was especially endowed with powers of wisdom to inherit
the leadership of the Jewish people. Before the twins were
born, God had already told her: "Two nations are in your
womb. . . . One people shall be mightier than the other, and
the older shall serve the younger." Rebekah was simply following her inner voice, favoring the younger child she
sensed would be the leader.

Nahum Sarna: "Two nations are in your womb . . . and
the older shall serve the younger." (Genesis 25:23) The Bible
is not condoning what has been obtained by trickery. On the
contrary, the way the narrative is handled makes clear that
Jacob has a claim on the birthright wholly and solely by
virtue of God's predetermination. In other words, the pres-

ence of the oracle in the story constitutes, in effect, a moral judgment upon Jacob's behavior.

Abarbanel: "When Isaac was old and his eyes were dim" (Genesis 27:1) There is no doubt that Isaac should have given thought to Esau's character, his wickedness, and that of his wives, and the likelihood that his children would follow their father's bad example. He should have prayed to God for guidance as to whether he should bless the eldest or the most deserving. Affection, however, ruins one's power of judgment. His affection for Esau blinded him to his faults. That is the implication of the phrase: "When Isaac was old, and his eyes were dim." His powers of judgment grew dim and he was not able to see reality.

David Kimchi: Why was Isaac insistent on blessing Esau? Kimchi posits that Isaac knew Esau's weakness and hoped that the blessing would help him to mend his ways.

Umberto Cassuto: Blessings, like curses, are ultimately prayers that God might translate them into reality, even as the Psalmist says: "Let them curse, but bless You." To be sure, there are scholars who see in the Bible, and especially in the blessing of Isaac, instances of magic, in that what has been said cannot be taken back. However, here too we have not magic but prayer, for it was not Isaac's intention to force God to do something against God's will. The blessing cannot stand unless it represents God's will to begin with.

Samuel E. Karff: Apparently even God must select imperfect instruments to fulfill God's purposes. God must choose between Jacob—a man who desires the birthright so deeply that he will cheat to secure it—and Esau, who so lightly esteems it that he forfeits the birthright for a bowl of lentils. Jacob's calculated cunning must be weighted against Esau's undisciplined craving for immediate self-gratification. Working with "human material" involved God in a difficult but inescapable choice, and God decides: It is better to care too much than too little.

Genesis Rabbah 65:19: "Isaac said to his son, 'How did you succeed so quickly, my son?'" (Genesis 27:20) The moment Isaac heard his son mention God's name (Genesis 27:20), he knew it was Jacob, and not Esau.

Questions

1. Why does the Bible tell us that "Esau despised his birthright"?

2. Why does the Bible mention that Esau sold his birthright to Jacob but fail to mention anything about Jacob "buying" the birthright from him?

3. What do you think the Bible might have meant when it said: "Isaac's eyes were dim, and he could not see"?

4. Did Isaac know who Jacob was when he (Jacob) dressed up to look like Esau? Prove it from the text.

5. In your opinion, was Jacob's behavior unethical? In the opinion of the Bible, was his behavior unethical?

6. The rabbis occasionally permitted white lies, especially those intended to promote peace and harmony. Can you think of an occasion in your life when you altered the truth for the sake of peace?

7. Jacob is the third of the three patriarchs. How does it make you feel to know that he engaged in deception?

8. A very perplexing aspect of this Bible story is Isaac's insistence that he cannot withdraw the blessing from Jacob once he had given it to him and restore it to Esau. The Torah never explains why a blessing given under false pretenses cannot be reassigned to its proper recipient. Can you explain Isaac's actions?

9. The Torah still seems to be troubled by Jacob's deception of his father Isaac. For later, when Jacob falls in love with his cousin Rachel, and arranges to marry her, his uncle Laban deceives him by substituting his older daughter Leah, under a heavy veil. Many commentators have noted the parallel: Just as Jacob deceived his father, so is he deceived. Still later in the Book of Genesis, Jacob is deceived by his ten sons, who trick him into thinking that his eleventh son, Joseph, has

been killed by a savage beast. What do you think is the role that deception plays in the Bible? Is the Bible trying to teach us something? Are there circumstances when deception ought to be permissible? If so, what are they?

10. The talmudic tractate called *Baba Metzia* 23b–24a observes that a scholar will never tell a lie except in three instances. Research this passage and see whether you agree with the talmudic sages.

IV. The Ten Commandments

How does God reveal God's will to people?

The Bible Story (Exodus 19 & 20)

Chapter 19

9. . . . God said to Moses: "I come to you in a thick cloud, that the people may hear when I speak with you, and may also believe you forever." . . . 10. And God said to Moses: "Go to the people and sanctify them today and tomorrow, and let them wash their garments. 11. Be ready against the third day, for God will come down in the sight of all the people upon mount Sinai." . . . 14. And Moses went down from the mount and sanctified the people and they washed their garments. . . . 16. And it came to pass that there were thunders and lightnings and a thick cloud upon the mount, and the voice of a very loud horn, and all the people that were in the camp trembled. . . . 18. Now Mount Sinai was altogether on smoke, because God descended upon it in fire. . . . 23. And Moses said to God: "The people cannot come up to Mount Sinai, for you did charge us saying: Set bounds about the mount, and sanctify it."

Chapter 20

1. And God spoke all these words saying: 2. I am God who brought you out of the land of Egypt, out of the house of bondage. 3. You shall worship only Me. 4. You shall not make a graven image to worship; 5. you shall not bow down to idols or serve them. . . . 7. You shall not use the name of God to take a false oath. 8. Observe the Sabbath day to keep it holy. . . . 12. Honor your father and your mother, that you may long endure on the land.

13. You shall not murder.

You shall not commit adultery.

You shall not steal.

You shall not bear false witness against your neighbor.

14. You shall not covet your neighbor's wife, and you shall not covet your neighbor's house, or field, or servant, or anything that belongs to your neighbor.

15. And all the people perceived the thunderings, and the voice of the horn, and the mountains smoking. And when the people saw it, they trembled and stood far away.

The Problem

Three months after entering the Sinai desert, Moses and the Israelites camp at Mount Sinai. Moses goes up to the top of the mountain, and God speaks to him, giving him the Ten Commandments. Below, the people hear thunder and see lightning. They remain at a distance while Moses communes with God.

The giving of the Ten Commandments is one of the most important events in Jewish history. It is also clearly a moment filled with mystery. The Torah reports that while the Israelites stood at the bottom of the mountain, they not only saw smoke and fire rising but heard the blare of horns and felt the whole mountain quaking violently. According to the report, the people were so frightened that they remained below while Aaron and Moses climbed to the top. Afterwards, Moses descended and presented the Ten Commandments to the people.

From that moment until today, Jews have asked the question: "What really happened at Mount Sinai?" How did God speak to Moses and what did the people actually hear? Is the Torah report an accurate reporting of history or a legend in which some kernels of truth are hidden?

There are many differing views about what happened at Mount Sinai. For example, Rabbi Yochanan posits that God's voice was divided into seven voices, and the seven voices were further subdivided into the seventy languages spoken by all the peoples of the world at that time.

According to the talmudic tractate of *Megillah* (19b), when the Torah was given, God showed Moses all the details of the Torah and all the innovations that would later be introduced by the rabbis. In other words, Moses had a sort of "sneak peak" into the future!

Some of the ancient rabbis claimed that God gave two Torahs to Moses. One they called *Torah shebeechtav*, the "Written Torah," comprising the Five Books of Moses. The other they called *Torah Shebe'al peh*, the "Oral Torah," made up of all the books of the prophets, the *Midrash Aggadah* of the Talmud, and all decisions and explanations of Jewish law by rabbis through the ages.

Today there are still Orthodox Jews who believe that God revealed His will at Mount Sinai both in written and oral form. Exactly how the communication between God and the Israelites took place is a mystery. But for the Orthodox, the fact remains that the Torah was revealed verbally (i.e. using words) directly to the people. Thus, God spoke words and the people directly received God's communication.

In Conservative Judaism, the nature of God's communication has been understood in various ways. For some, God communicated with mortals both at Sinai and in the era of the prophets. These revelations were written down by human beings, and thus the writings included in the Bible are of diverse origins. The authority of Jewish law is based upon the fact that it is God's will, as stated first in the Torah and then by the rabbis of each generation.

Another Conservative position holds that human beings were divinely inspired with specific messages at various places and times in our history. This position combines divine inspiration and human articulation.

In yet a third Conservative position, the Torah is understood as the human record of the encounter between God and the Jews. The Torah was written by human beings to whom God disclosed Himself, but without declaring specific rules or ideas. This position emphasizes the responsibility of rabbis to make appropriate changes in the tradition which accurately reflect God's will in the contemporary world.

Reconstructionist Jews generally posit that human beings wrote the Torah, claiming no divinity for the product. Rabbinic authorities representing the community in each generation have an obligation to reconstruct Judaism with meaningful customs and ideas. Jewish law has authority as the folkways and customs of the Jewish people. When a particular law becomes offensive or falls into disuse, it should be changed or modified.

The Reform position maintains that the Torah is God's will as written by human beings. Often called "progressive revelation," this position holds that as time goes on, people will be better able to understand God's will. Each person must decide both what and how to obey, and each is allowed personal autonomy.

To conclude, we do not know, nor can anyone really ever know, exactly what Moses or the people at Sinai actually heard, saw or felt. Many of the words used in the Bible's description of revelation are figurative. It is your task to begin to formulate your own understanding of how God revealed His will to an entire people. As you continue to think and answer the questions that will shortly follow, you may begin to see the development of your own personal faith statements. Ultimately this understanding should assist you in deciding how to interpret and act upon the laws, customs and rituals that are found both in the Bible and in rabbinic Judaism.

What the Commentaries Say

Judah HaLevi: The people believed that Moses held direct communication with God, that his words were not creations of his own mind. They did not believe Moses had seen a vision in sleep, or that someone had spoken with him between sleeping and waking so that he only heard the words in his imagination but not with his ears, that he saw a phantom and afterwards pretended that God had spoken with him.

David Hartman: The Torah given at Mount Sinai was not a complete, finished system. Belief in the giving of the Torah at Sinai does not necessarily imply that the full truth has already been given and that our task is only to unfold what was already present in the fullness of the founding moment of revelation. What happened at Mount Sinai gave the community a direction, an arrow pointing toward a future filled with many surprises. The Sinai moment of revelation invites one and all to acquire the competence to explore the terrain and extend the road.

Jakob Petuchowski: "On the third day, as morning came, there was thunder and lightning." (Exodus 19:16) The thunders and lightnings at Sinai, as they appear in the biblical narrative, are an echo sounding through the ages of what had happened there. They testify to the fact of revelation, to the impact it had on the people. But it is only the man of a prosaic mind, the man lacking in imagination, who would

read this biblical account as if it were a news bulletin reporting in every detail what has actually happened.

Franz Rosenzweig: The people did not hear words spoken at Mount Sinai at all. What happened there and what left
a lasting impression is that people encountered God. It was
at Sinai that the people began the process of searching out
what God wanted of them.

Abraham Joshua Heschel: A cosmic fear enveloped all
those who stood at Sinai, a moment more staggering than the
heart could feel. What we see may be an illusion. *That* we see
can never be questioned. The thunder and lightning at Sinai
may have been merely an impression. But to have suddenly
been endowed with the power of seeking the whole world
struck with an overwhelming awe of God was a new sort of
perception. Only in moments when we are able to share in
the spirit of awe that fills the world are we able to understand what happened to Israel at Sinai.

Philo: The voice of men is calculated to be heard. But that
of God to be really and truly seen. Why? Because all that God
says are not words, but actions which the eyes perceive but
the ears do.

Exodus Rabbah: ". . . that the people may hear when I
speak to you." (Exodus 19:9) Each Israelite heard what was
in his/her power to hear.

Questions

1. Do you believe that God has ever spoken or still speaks to people? What do people hear?

2. Maimonides, the medieval philosopher, wrote Thirteen Principles of Faith. One of them states: I believe that all the words of the Torah are true. How close does this principle come to your own beliefs?

3. Do you believe that God still reveals His will to people? Has God ever revealed something to you? If so, share it with your classmates.

4. What was the purpose in the Bible story of the shofar, the smoke and the quaking of the mountain?

5. Compare the version of the Ten Commandments in the Book of Exodus with the other version of the Ten Commandments in the fifth chapter of the Book of Deuteronomy. What are the major differences?

6. Scholars have noted that there is a logical structure to the Ten Commandments. Compare the first five commandments with the last five in terms of their themes.

7. It is generally assumed that the two tablets upon which were written the Ten Commandments were of equal size. Pictorially the commandments are generally portrayed five

on one tablet and five on the other tablet. Let's do some biblical arithmetic. All told there are 172 words in the Ten Commandments. The first five commandments consist of 146 words and the second five only 26 words. Thus, the second tablet would easily have been one fifth of the first tablet. Why then did God give Moses two tablets, one with 146 words and the other with 26 words?

8. Of the Ten Commandments, which commandment do you think is the most difficult to follow? Why?

9. Which view of revelation according to the commentators do you find the most personally satisfying? The least satisfying? Why?

10. What are the unifying factors that unite all of the positions on revelation in this chapter?

V. The Sin of the Golden Calf

The Bible Story (Exodus 32:1–35)

1. When the people saw that Moses was taking so long in coming down from the mountain, they congregated against Aaron and said to him: "Come, make for us a god who shall go before us, for that Moses, we do not know what has happened to him." 2. Aaron said to them: "Remove the rings that are on the ears of your wives, your sons, your daughters, and bring them to me."

3. All the people removed their gold rings that were in their ears and brought them to Aaron. 4. He took them from them and cast them in a mold and made into it a molten calf. And they exclaimed: "This is your god, O Israel, who brought you out of the land of Egypt." 5. When Aaron saw this, he built an altar before it. And Aaron announced: "Tomorrow shall be a festival of God."

6. Early next day the people offered up burnt offerings and brought sacrifices of well-being. They sat down to eat and drink, and then they rose up to dance.

7. God spoke to Moses: "Hurry down, for your people, whom you brought out of the land of Egypt, have acted basely. 8. They have been hasty to turn aside from the way that I

instructed them. They have made themselves a molten calf and bowed low to it and sacrificed to it, saying: 'This is your god, O Israel, who brought you out of the land of Egypt." 9. God further said to Moses: "I see that this is a stiffnecked people. 10. Now, let Me be, that My anger may blaze forth, against them that I may destroy them, and make of you a great nation." 11.But Moses implored God saying: "Let not Your anger blaze forth against Your people, whom You delivered out of Egypt with great power. 12. Let not the Egyptians say: 'It was with evil intent that God delivered them, only to kill them off in the mountains.' Turn from Your blazing anger and renounce the plan to punish Your people. 13. Remember Your servants Abraham, Isaac and Jacob, how You swore to them and said to them: I will make your off-spring as numerous as the stars of heaven, and I will give to your offspring this whole land of which I spoke, to possess forever." 14. And God relinquished the punishment God had planned to bring upon His people. . . .

19. As soon as Moses came near to the camp and saw the calf and the dancing, he became enraged. He hurled the tablets from his hands and shattered them at the foot of the mountain. 20. He took the calf that they had made and burned it. He ground it to powder and strewed it upon the water and so made the Israelites drink it.

21. Moses said to Aaron: "What did this people do to you that you have brought such great sin upon them?" 22. Aaron said: Let not my lord be angry. You know that this people is bent on evil. 23. They said to me: 'Make us a god to lead us, for that man Moses who brought us from the land of Egypt,

we do not know what has happened to him.' 24. So I said to them, 'Whoever has gold, take it off.' They gave it to me and I hurled it into the fire and out came this calf." 25. Moses saw that the people were out of control—since Aaron had let them get out of control—so that they were a menace to any who might oppose them. 26. Moses stood up in the gate of the camp and said: "Whoever is for God, come here." And all the Levites rallied to him.

27. He said to them, "Thus says God. Each of you put sword on thigh, go back and forth from gate to gate throughout the camp, and slay brother, neighbor and kin." 28. The Levites did as Moses had bidden. Some three thousand people fell that day. 29. And Moses said: "Consecrate yourselves to God this day, for each of you has been against son and brother— that God may bestow a blessing upon you today."

30. The next day Moses said to the people,"You have been guilty of a great sin. Yet I will now go up to God. Perhaps I may win forgiveness for your sin." 31. Moses went back to God and said: "This people is guilty of a great sin in making for themselves a god of gold. 32. Now, if You will forgive their sin, well and good. If not, erase me from the record which You have written." 33. But God said to Moses, "He who has sinned against Me, him only will I erase from My record. 34. Go forth and lead the people where I told you. See, My angel shall go before you. But when I make an accounting, I will bring them to account for their sins." 35. Then God sent a plague upon the people, for what they did with the calf that Aaron made.

The Problem

The incident of the golden calf left deep scars on the memory of Israel. Nothing would be quite the same thereafter, and a midrash (Exodus Rabbah 43:2) says that all the ills which have befallen the people since that time are in part traceable to the sin of the golden calf.

While Moses remains on Mount Sinai, the Israelites protest to Aaron, asking him to make them a golden calf, an idol to worship. Surprisingly, this Aaron does, and the Israelites offer sacrifices before the calf and sit down to drink and make merry.

God tells Moses what the people have done and threatens to destroy them. Moses intercedes and argues with God to show compassion. His argument convinces God not to punish the people.

Holding the tablets, Moses comes down the mountain. When he sees the Israelites dancing before the golden calf, he shatters the tablets on the ground and burns the calf. He grinds the calf to powder, sprinkles water on it and forces the Israelites to drink it.

Aaron immediately blames the people, explaining that they requested the idol. He also explains to Moses that he told them to give their gold, which he threw "into the fire and out came this calf."

Judging that the people are out of control, Moses calls upon all who are loyal to God to join him. All of the Levites come forward and following his direction, kill those who have demonstrated disloyalty to God. In addition, a plague is sent among the people as punishment for the sin of creating the golden calf.

Many questions and problems have been raised in this Bible story. How could the Israelites revert so quickly to idolatry. Why did Aaron acquiesce to the people's demands? Why would Moses hurl the holy commandments to the ground? Was this being a good role model for the people?

What the Commentaries Say

Exodus Rabbah 42:3: The real sin lay not in the making of the golden calf but in what Israel thought and said when Moses failed to return. Israel said: God redeemed only himself but not us. God is concerned with himself but not with us.

A. Schoenberg: While Aaron wants to express the idea of God by an understandable image, Moses demands unconditional surrender to an almighty invisible deity. Aaron is convinced that the people will not believe in a god they cannot see. It is the clash between the ideal that the crowd needs to worship and the pure idea of deity—the collision between corporeality and spirituality. When Moses rebukes Aaron because he has tainted the purity of the faith, Aaron points out that the tablets Moses is carrying are also corporeal corruptions of total purity. In sudden despair Moses smashes the tablets, whereupon Aaron rebukes him because the tablets would have helped Israel's faith.

Exodus Rabbah 43:1: ". . . he hurled the tablets from his hands and shattered them." (Exodus 32:19) Moses broke the tablets out of his love for Israel, for as long as they did not know the Torah they would be judged less harshly. God consoled him, saying: The second tablets will contain much more material—*halacha, midrash* and *aggadah.*

Martin Buber: "Let us make a god who shall go before us, for that man Moses . . . we do not know what happened to him." (Exodus 32:1) He asserts that the Israelites were in a state of panic and said to one another: Moses has completely vanished. It must be supposed that God of his has made away with him. What are we to do now? We must take matters into our own hands. An image has to be made, and then the power of God will enter the image and there will be proper guidance.

Judah HaLevi: He held that only 3,000 of the 600,000 people actually requested that Aaron build the golden calf. These people were not really idolaters. In the absence of Moses, they were simply desperate to have a tangible object of worship like the other nations without repudiating God who had brought them out of Egypt. Having waited so long, the Israelites were overcome with frustration and confusion. As a result, they divided into angry parties. No longer able to control their fears, a vocal minority pressured Aaron into taking their gold and casting it into a golden calf.

Furthermore, HaLevi argues, the creation of the golden calf was not such a serious sin. After all, he explains, making images and using them for worship was accepted religious practice during ancient times. God had commanded the people to create the cherubim and place them above the ark. If the people made a mistake, HaLevi says, it was not in refusing to worship God, but in their impatience.

Adin Steinsaltz: "Aaron said to them, 'Take off the gold rings on the ears of your wives . . .'" (Exodus 32:2) He labels the episode of the golden calf the worst failure of Aaron's career. Aaron's guiding principle is peace at any price, compromise to avoid confrontation. For that reason, he offers no argument when the people tell him to create an idol. He desperately wants to be loved and to be popular.

Nechama Leibowitz: She sees in the golden calf story not only Aaron's failure or the sin of the Israelites, but a conscious warning that human beings are capable of acting nobly at one moment and ugly at the next. One single religious experience (i.e. The Ten Commandments) was not capable of changing the people from idol worshipers to monotheists. Only a lengthy disciplining in the laws of Torah could accomplish a true change.

Exodus Rabbah 42:10: ". . . perhaps I may win forgiveness for your sin." (Exodus 32:30) Rav Huna believes that Moses intervened on Israel's behalf because he was convinced that their worshiping the golden calf was actually God's fault. The people had not chosen to live among idolaters in Egypt. God had placed them in that evil environment where they had learned bad habits. They were thus incapable of overcoming the conditions in which they had been reared as children and had survived as adults.

Rabbi Meyer Simcha of Dvinsk: "he hurled the tablets from his hands and shattered them . . ." (Exodus 32:19) He teaches that no object is intrinsically holy. A Torah written by a heretic must be burned, because in the final analysis, it is the person who endows an object with holiness or profanity. Worshiping an idol, in effect, tainted the heart of the Jews. Since it is the Jews who sanctify Torah, their idolatry stripped the tablets of their sacred quality. By breaking them, Moses was demonstrating our responsibility for the sanctity of Torah.

Rashi: "he hurled the tablets from his hands and shattered them . . . "(Exodus 32:19) He quotes a discussion in the talmudic tractate of *Shabbat* 87a, which makes the point that worshiping the golden calf made Israel strangers to the entire Torah. "If the Passover sacrifice, which is but one of the 613 mitzvot, cannot be partaken by a stranger, since the Torah said no stranger shall eat of it, how much more is it true that the whole Torah may not be partaken of by the Israelites when the Israelites are apostates (strangers to it)." Strangers to the Torah do not need, or want, the tablets, so Moses breaks them.

Rashbam: " . . . he hurled the tablets from his hands and shattered them." (Exodus 32:19) He suggests that when

Moses comes upon the Israelites with the golden calf, his strength vanishes. It isn't so much anger as a profoundly bitter sadness that causes Moses to smash the tablets.

Kli Yakar: ". . . he hurled the tablets from his hands and shattered them." (Exodus 32:19) He says that the tablets are witnesses to a divine revelation between God and Israel, thus publicizing the enormity of their sin. Moses does not want his people to suffer, so he breaks the tablets to mute their testimony.

Questions

1. Why were the Israelites so impatient with Moses? Why do you think they wished to revert so quickly to producing their own god?

2. What's your reaction to Aaron's decision to immediately begin to work for the people by asking for a collection of jewelry?

3. What are Moses' compelling arguments to God in order to convince God not to lay harm on to the Israelites? How do they relate to Moses as leader of the people?

4. Why did Moses cast the tablets to the ground? Was this being a good role model for the people?
5. How would you rate Aaron's leadership in this story? Did he demonstrate weak or clever leadership?

6. How do fear and frustration cause a people to abandon democracy or freedom?

7. Does society today worship idols? What are our modern-day golden calfs?

8. Which commentator's opinion of why the Israelites needed the golden calf is most like your own?

9. The Zohar suggests that idolatry occurring so soon after the Exodus and Sinai reveals to Moses a flaw in his leadership. If the people could sink this low, part of the blame must fall on his own shoulders, and certainly every leader is responsible for training and elevating someone to take his place when he is absent. Moses neglected to do this, and his breaking of the tablets is perhaps his way of sharing in the Israelites' sin, and therefore punishment. How do you react to the suggestion of the Zohar? Do you think Moses bears blame for this tragic story?

VI. Leprosy
Biblical medicine, ritual and ethics

The Bible Story (Leviticus 12:1–6, 13:1–6, 45, 46; 14:2–12, 20)

Chapter 12

1. God spoke to Moses, saying: 2. Speak to the Israelite people: When a woman at childbirth bears a male, she shall be unclean seven days; she shall be unclean at the time of her menstrual infirmity. . . . 5. If she bears a female, she shall be unclean two weeks as during her menstruation. . . .

6. On the completion of her period of purification, for either son or daughter, she shall bring to the priest a lamb in its first year for a burnt offering, and a pigeon or a turtledove for a sin offering.

Chapter 13

1. God spoke to Moses and Aaron saying: 2. When a person has on the skin of his body a swelling, a rash, or a discoloration, and it develops into a scaly affection on the skin of his body, it shall be reported to Aaron the priest or to one

of his sons, the priests. 3. The priest shall examine the infection on the skin of his body. 4. If hair on the affected patch has turned white and the affection appears to be deeper than the skin of his body, it is a leprous affection. When the priest sees it, he shall pronounce him unclean. 4. But if it is a white discoloration on the skin of his body which does not appear to be deeper than the skin and the hair in it has not turned white, the priest shall isolate the affected person for seven days. 5. On the seventh day the priest shall examine him, and if the affection remains unchanged in color and the disease has not spread on the skin, the priest shall isolate him for another seven days. 6. On the seventh day the priest shall examine him again. If the affection has faded and has not spread on the skin, the priest shall pronounce him clean. . . .

45. As for the person with a leprous affection, his clothes shall be rent, his hair shall be left bare, and he shall cover his upper lip. 46. And he shall call out, "Unclean, unclean." Being unclean he shall dwell apart, outside the camp.

Chapter 14

2. This shall be the ritual for a leper at the time he is to be cleansed. When it has been reported to the priest, 3. the priest shall go outside the camp. If the priest sees that the leper has healed his scaly affection, 4. the priest shall order two live clean birds, cedar wood, crimson stuff and hyssop to be brought for him who is to be cleaned. 5. The priest shall order one of the birds slaughtered over fresh water in an earthen vessel. 6. And he shall take the live bird, along with the cedar

wood, the crimson stuff, the hyssop and dip them together with the live bird in the blood of the bird that was killed over the fresh water. 7. He shall then sprinkle it seven times on him who is to be cleansed of the eruption and cleanse him. And he shall set the live bird free in the open country. 8. The one to be cleansed shall wash his clothes, shave off all his hair, and bathe in water. Then he shall be clean. After that he may enter the camp, but he must remain outside his tent seven days. 9. On the seventh day he shall shave off all his hair, wash his clothes and bathe his body in water. Then he shall be clean. 10. On the eighth day he shall take two male lambs without blemish, one ewe lamb in its first year without blemish, three tenths of a measure of choice flour with oil mixed in for a meal offering, and one log of oil. 11. These shall be presented before God, with the man to be cleansed, at the entrance of the Tent of Meeting, by the priest who performs the cleansing. 12. The priest shall take one of the male lambs and offer it with the log of oil as a guilt offering, and he shall wave them as a wave offering before God. . . . 20. The priest shall offer the burnt offering and the meal offering on the altar, and the priest shall make expiation for him. Then he shall be clean.

The Problem

Leprosy was the most dreaded disease in Bible times. In the Bible this disease, called *tzara'at* in Hebrew, designates a variety of skin ailments. It is also applied to unusual changes in the appearance of fabrics and of house walls.

For the biblical authors, leprosy was a *nega*, a smiting, the manifestation of extreme divine pleasure. That is to say, when one became afflicted with leprosy, it was believed that it was due to God's anger. In addition, unlike others forms of defilement, it does not merely exclude the defiled person from the sanctuary. Rather, it bars that person from all of human society. It is likely that the emotional overtones attached to biblical leprosy contributed to the sense of horror and revulsion which the very word "leprosy" evokes today in Western culture.

Regarding leprosy as a plague, the expression of God's anger, it was natural to inquire what sin evokes this punishment. Numerous stories in the Bible suggest that it might be brought on by several different sins. Miriam, sister of Moses, was punished for her unjustified criticism of Moses by a brief attack of the ailment. (Numbers 12:10) King Uzziah in the Second Book of Chronicles (26:16) had the effrontery to offer incense on the inner altar, whereupon leprosy broke out on his forehead.

A variety of opinions is also offered by the rabbis. A favorite device of midrashic preachers was to pun on the words *metzora* (leper) and *motzi ra* (slanderer). Thus, they utilized the reading of the Torah section on leprosy as an occasion to preach against hostile talk, slander and gossip.

Why does this Bible spend so much time detailing the disease of leprosy and the many rituals attached to it? Is it possible that God would intentionally smite a transgressor with this disease?

What the Commentaries Say

Maimonides: He maintains that leprosy is not a natural phenomenon but rather a sign and wonder for the people of Israel to warn them against *leshon hara*—evil talk.

Sforno: ". . . the priest shall isolate him for another seven days." (Exodus 13:5) He enlarges upon Maimonides's observation, arguing that the quarantine ordered by the priest is meant to prompt a person to ask God's forgiveness for his or her sins. The quarantine is a time to reconsider one's actions, both the intentional and unintentional ones. In confronting one's shortcomings, honestly scrutinizing one's treatment of others, there is a chance for personal improvement and repentance. In this way the affliction of leprosy leads to isolation, which leads to repentance, which brings about God's forgiveness for wrongdoing and the rehabilitation of each sinful human being.

Nechama Lebowitz: She holds that the plague of leprosy teaches us that society should take notice of the first sign of misconduct, however small. Just the same as a disease begins with hardly noticeable symptoms and can be stopped if detected in time, so a moral disease in society can be prevented from spreading if immediate steps are taken. Otherwise, it will spread throughout the community.

Rashbam: He posits that since the plague of leprosy was a punishment for slander, arrogance and greed, even a king who became leprous had to humble himself and turn to the priest for guidance on how to repent of his sin and thus cure himself of the illness.

Kli Yakar: Leprosy is caused by slander, a sin in which the transgressor projects his own shortcomings onto his victim. The purpose of the procedure of purification to be undergone by the leper was to force him to face reality and examine his own shortcomings before slandering another.

Talmud Arachin 16a: ". . . the priest shall order two live clean birds. . . . The priest shall order one of the birds slaughtered." (Leviticus 14:4–5) Why does the sin offering of those with skin diseases consist of birds? Because the sin of such persons is gossip. They are "chirping" all the time. Therefore, their offering must remind them of their wrongdoing—warn them of how dangerous it is to engage in gossip.

Magid of Dubno: Jews often treat the sin of slander lightly, as they do not realize the tremendous power of the mouth. They do not understand the harm that slander can cause. After all, they think to themselves: "What have I done? All I did was say a few words." The person is therefore brought to the priest, and there he sees that it is the words of the priest which determine his fate: whether he will be considered clean or unclean. He realizes what power words do indeed have. "Death and life are in the control of the tongue."

Questions

1. Who examines the person with the skin blemish? Why do you think the Torah specifies this person? Why can't just anybody do the examination?

2. What is the goal of the examination?

3. What are the rituals that the leprous person must perform?

4. Why must the leper call out "unclean, unclean"? How do you think this made the person feel? Did it help or hurt them?

5. How might individuals in the community have reacted?

6. Why does the leper have to dwell outside the camp?

7. Why does the person have to be cleansed if the disease of leprosy is already healed?

8. What is the purpose of the entire purification ritual?

9. Who in your estimation are today's modern-day lepers?

10. Why do you think that so many rabbis connected the sin of leprosy with slander and gossip? What is so abhorrent about slander?

11. What is the purpose of the elaborate ritual ceremonies related to the purification of the leper?

12. Here are some verses in the Bible related to the power of the tongue. Read and discuss them with your teacher.

There are those who speak like the piercings of a sword. But the tongue of the wise is health. (Proverbs 12:18)

A lying tongue hates those who are hurt by it. And a flattering mouth works ruin. (Proverbs 26:28)

A soft answer turns away anger, but grievous words stir up anger. (Proverbs 15:1)

13. Here are some selected phrases from the *Al Het* confessional prayer recited on Yom Kippur. Read them to determine what many of them have in common. What is the common thread that runs through many of them? What does it tell us about what the rabbis felt were the most common sins of people:

We have missed the mark—

by being heartless   *by deceit and falsehood*
by the wrong way we speak   *by gossiping*

by wronging our neighbor
by confessing insincerely
by mocking parents
by foul language
by not keeping promises

by the way we eat and drink
by judging others too quickly
by being selfish teachers
by foolish talk

14. In the *Elohai Netzor* prayer that concludes the *Amidah*, there is a line that says, "To those who slander me, let me give no heed." Is it possible to ignore someone who slanders you? How would you explain this verse?

15. A Hasidic teaching states that "human beings are God's language." How would you interpret this teaching?

VII. Ten Spies
Demoralizing a people

The Bible Story (Numbers 13:1, 2, 17–20, 25–33; Numbers 14:1–2, 3–12, 26, 30, 36–38)

Chapter 13

1. God spoke to Moses: 2. Send men that they may scout the land of Canaan which I am giving to the Israelite people. Send one man from each of their ancestral tribes. . . . 17. When Moses sent them to scout the land of Canaan, he said to them: "Go up there to the Negev and to the hill country. 18. See what kind of country it is. Are the people who live there strong or weak, few or many? 19. Is the country in which they dwell strong or weak, few or many? Is the country in which they live good or bad? Are the towns they live in open or fortified? 20. Is the soil rich or poor? Is it wooded or not? And take pains to bring back some of the fruit of the land. . . .

25. At the end of forty days they returned from scouting the land. 26. They went directly to Moses and Aaron and the whole Israelite community at Kadesh in the wilderness of Paran, and they gave their report to them and to the entire

community, as they showed them the fruit of the land. 27. This is what they told him: "We came to the land you sent us to; it does indeed flow with milk and honey, and this is its fruit. 28. But the people who inhabit the land are powerful, and the cities are fortified and very large. 29. Moreover, we saw the Anakites there. Amalekites dwell in the Negev region; Hittites, Jebusites and Amorites live in the hill country. And Canaanites dwell by the Sea and along the Jordan." 30. Caleb quieted the people before Moses and said: "Let's by all means go up and gain possession of the land, for we shall certainly overcome it." 31. But the men who had gone up with him said: "We cannot attack that people, for it is stronger than we." 32. Thus they spread calumnies among the Israelites about the land that they scouted, saying, "The country that we traversed and scouted is one that devours its settlers. All the people that we saw in it are giants. 33. We saw the Nephilim there—the Anakites are part of the Nephilim, and we looked like grasshoppers to ourselves, and so we must have looked to them."

Chapter 14

1. The whole community broke into loud cries, and the people cried all night. 2. All the Israelites complained to Moses: "If only we had died in Egypt," the whole community shouted at them, "or if only we might die in this wilderness. 3. Why is God taking us to that land to fall by the sword? . . . 4. And they said to one another: "Let us go back to Egypt."

5. Then Moses and Aaron fell on their faces before all the Israelites. 6. And Joshua son of Nun and Caleb son of Jephunneh, of those who had scouted the land, rent their clothing and 7. admonished the whole Israelite community saying: "The land that we traversed and scouted is a very good land. 8. If God is pleased with us, God will bring us into that land, a land flowing with milk and honey, and give it to us. 9. Only you must not rebel against God. Have no fear of the people of the country, for they are our prey. Their protection has departed from them, but God is with us. Be not afraid of them. "

10. As the whole community threatened to throw stones at them, God appeared in the Tent of Meeting to all of the Israelites. 11. And God said to Moses: "How long will this people spurn Me, and how long will they have no faith in Me despite all the signs that I have given them? 12. I will strike you with pestilence." . . .

26. God further spoke to Moses and Aaron: "How much longer shall that wicked community keep muttering against Me? . . . 30. Not one shall enter the land in which I swore to settle you, except for Caleb son of Jephunneh and Joshua son of Nun.

36. As for the men who Moses sent to spy out the land, who came back and caused the whole community to mutter against him by spreading lies about the land. 37. Those who spread such lies about the land died of plague, by the will of God.

38. Of those men who had gone to scout the land, only Joshua son of Nun and Caleb son of Jephunneh survived.

The Problem

This story, perhaps the most famous spy story in the entire Bible, describes how the twelve spies, each of whom represented one of the tribes of Israel, scouted the Land of Israel. After forty days they return. Ten of the spies report that although the land is fruitful, its cities are filled with powerful giants, making the people in comparison to them look like grasshoppers. The report terrifies the community. Seeking to assure the Israelites, Caleb says that by all means the people should go up and gain possession of the land, for they will surely win any battles that will come their way.

It is then that the entire community turns on Moses and Aaron, suggesting that all return back to Egypt. At that point, Joshua and Caleb try to reassure the community that the land is exceedingly good, and with faith in God they will surely defeat the enemy. Rejecting this advice, the people threaten to pelt them with stones. It is at this point that God then tells Moses that none shall enter the Promised Land, except for Caleb and Jephunneh.

What was the sin of the spies? And what was the sin of the response of the people to the spies that so very much angered God? There are many commentaries that attempt to answer these questions.

What the Commentaries Say

Aaron Wildavsky: In his study *Moses as a Political Leader*, Aaron Wildavsky suggests that the sin of the spies is more serious than the heinous sin of slander. The Israelites have left Egypt with the promise of conquering the Land of Israel. That is their goal. The spies return and take advantage of the people's anticipation of their report to "discredit the entire enterprise." That is their sin. They conspire to convince the people that God is leading them to disaster. Thus they essentially kill the hopes of their people, and thus their generation is condemned to wander and die in the desert.

Isaac Arama: He suggests that the sin of the spies was their rejection of the Land of Israel. They scorn and spurn the Land of Israel and rally the people to tell Moses to take them back to Egypt. For this reason (i.e. their disloyalty to the land), they are all condemned to die in the desert.

Yitzchak Meir of Ger: "The land which we have spied out is a land that devours its inhabitants, and all the people which we saw were powerful people." (numbers 13:32) He states that the sin of the spies is not their plan to undermine the expectations of the people to settle the land but their actual carrying out of the plan after their scouting mission. He asserts that people are not held responsible for evil thoughts or plans. Rather, they sin when they translate their evil plans into the reality of deeds. This is the essence of the sin of the spies. With their negative report they translate their evil plans into the reality of deeds.

Sforno: "All the people that we saw are men of great size . . . and we looked like grasshoppers to ourselves." (Numbers

14:32–33) He explains that when the spies mention the giants in their remarks, they mean to suggest that the climate of the land is so polluted that only the strongest of them will survive. Similarly, when they claim that 'they felt like grasshoppers, the spies are deliberately exaggerating the physical size of their enemies to frighten the people.

Pinchus Peli: ". . . the country that we traversed and scouted is one that devours its settlers." (Numbers 13:32) By observing that "it is a land that eats up its people." Peli argues that the spies are conducting a demoralizing campaign, deliberately deceiving the people with lies about the land they have just scouted.

Menachem Schneerson: ". . . the country that we traversed and scouted is one that devours its settlers." (Numbers 13:32) He asserts that the sin of the spies is in their deception of the people. He also points out that the spies mislead themselves. They are pious and good and worry about the spiritual life of their people. However, they fear that the people will enter the Land of Israel and become so entrenched in materialistic concerns, with feeding their families and building their homes, that they will have progressively less time and energy for the service of God. This, explains Schneerson, is what the spies mean when they said that "it is a land that eats up its inhabitants." Their sin is in misleading the people and themselves with their opinion.

Nachmanides (Ramban): ". . . we cannot attack that people, for it is stronger than we are." (Numbers 14:31) He contends that the spies do not present any false facts, nor do they really exaggerate what they say. They show the people the fruit of the land, and tell the truth about it. Their fault, he argues, is misunderstanding the goal of their mission and in their reporting about it. They are sent, says Nachmanides, on a reconnaissance mission, with the goal of bringing back strategic details on how best to conquer the land. Their sin is in the negative tone in which they convey the information. This tone panics the people and causes them to reject the conquering of the Land of Israel.

Shlomo Riskin: "Thus they spread calumnies among the Israelites about the land that they scouted, saying, 'The country that we traversed and scouted is one that devours its settlers. All the people that we saw in it are giants. We saw the Nephilim there—the Anakites are part of the Nephilim, and we looked like grasshoppers to ourselves, and so we must have looked to them.'" (Numbers 13:32–33) Riskin posits that the sin of the spies is in the order and sequence of their answering the questions that Moses asks them when first beginning the mission. Moses says to the spies: "See what kind of land it is. Are the people strong or weak? Is the inhabited area good or bad. Is the soil rich or without trees?" (Numbers 13:17–20). Moses anticipates that after scouting the land the spies will first respond to the questions about the land's inhabitants, and later about the land. The most important word in Moses's instruction is *vehit'chazaktem* (you shall be strong)—strengthened by bringing back the fruit of the land. Who will worry about the children of giants when the land itself yields large crops? But Moses' instructions are reversed. First the spies respond to the topography of the land. Yes, the land flows with milk and honey. Then their words turn grim and frightening when they speak about the giants that inhabit the land. According to Riskin, what the scouts should have done was begin with the grim (i.e. details about the inhabitants) and end with a report about the land itself and its amazing fruits. Heeding Moses' sequence of questions would have strengthened the nation. Instead, the spies turn what should have been a great moment into an infamous one. Thus, according to Riskin, what really counts is the last word!

Seymour Essrog: "All the people that we saw are men of great size . . . and we looked like grasshoppers to ourselves." (Numbers 13:32–33) He quotes the Midrash of Bamidbar Rabbah, which depicts God as being angry with the spies and challenging them: "How do you know what you looked like to them? Perhaps you appeared to them like angels?" Essrog posits that people often tend to underestimate themselves and demean their importance as people. That was the transgression of the spies. (i.e. not believing in themselves and the power of the people of Israel) It is important to remember that if we look upon ourselves as insignificant, others will often take us precisely at our own evaluation.

Numbers Rabbah 16:17: In their report the spies began by speaking well of the land, saying it flowed with milk and honey, and then they went off to talk of its bad points. According to the midrash, that is how slanderers talk about people.

Numbers Rabbah 16:23" All of the Israelites 21 years of age were condemned to die in the desert, even those who silently disagreed with the majority and favored Joshua and Caleb. Why? Because they did not speak up.

Questions

1. Why did God tell Moses to send spies who, God knew, would bring back a false report?

2. There are commentators who state that the sin of the spies was in the use of the word "but." "But, they said, "the people who live there are powerful, and the cities and the cities are fortified and very large." Had they left out the word "but," the spies would have stayed within the limits of a factual report. When they added the word "but," it was no more a factual account, but rather an attempt to sway public opinion. How do you react to this commentary? Do you agree or disagree?

3. Moses asks the spies to bring him clear and precise answers to these questions:
    i. see what the land is
    ii. see whether the people are weak or strong
    iii. see whether the land is good or bad

iv. see what the cities are like

v. see whether the land is fat or lean, wooded or not

Are there other questions that you would have added to this list? What are the questions that you think need to be answered when a person sets up to explore a place in which to make his or her home?

4. Do you believe that the spies in any way were repudiating their trust in God? Can you prove this from the Bible story itself?

5. According to the Bible story, it says that "the land is a land that eats up its inhabitants." (Numbers 13:32) If the land consumed its inhabitants, then how did there exist men of great stature?

6. Our sages once enunciated in a midrash this principle: "A lie, to succeed, must contain a grain of truth." How does this principle apply to our Bible story? To which specific verse can this principle be applied?

7. The spies said: "We were as grasshoppers in our eyes, and so we were in their sight." How did the spies know how they appeared in the sight of the inhabitants of the land?

8. Do you feel that God's punishment of the Israelites was commensurate with their crime? What was the sin of the Israelites? What, in your opinion, was the sin of the spies in this Bible story?

9. The Kotzker Rebbe asserts that the sin of the spies was their statement "we were in our own sight as grasshoppers and so were in their sight." The Rebbe continued his explanation by stating that one can understand their statement "we were in our own sight as grasshoppers," for that was the way they really saw themselves. However, what right did the spies have to say, "and so were in their sight"? What difference should it make how we appeared to them? What is your opinion of the Kotzker Rebbe's comments? Can you think of a contemporary example that would help to explain the Kotzker Rebbe's words?

10. Can you think of modern-day examples of the necessity for a person to "fudge the truth" for a greater cause?

11. What are the lessons that you have learned from the story of the spies?

12. Do you think that a Jew is disloyal if he/she spreads "an evil report" about the State of Israel?

VIII. Korach's Challenge to Moses' Leadership

Rebellion that is not for the sake of heaven

The Bible Story (Numbers 16:1–13, 16–32, 35)

1. Now Korach, son of Izhar son of Kohat, son of Levi, along with Datan and Aviram, 2. came to rise up against Moses along with two hundred and fifty Israelites.

3. They said to Moses and Aaron: "You have gone too far. For all of the community are holy, and God is in their midst. Why then do you raise yourselves above God's congregation? 4. When Moses heard this he fell on his face.

5. Then he spoke to Korach and all his company, saying:

"In the morning, God will make known who God is and who is holy, and will grant access to God. 6. Do this: You, Korach, and all of your band, take fire pans and 7. tomorrow put fire in them and lay incense upon them before God. Then the man whom God chooses, he shall be the holy one. You have gone too far, sons of Levi."

8. Moses further said to Korach: "Hear me, sons of Levi. 9. Is it not enough for you that God has set you apart from the community of Israel and has given you access to God, to

67

perform the duties of God's tabernacle and to minister to the community and serve them? 10. Now that God has advanced you and all of your fellow Levites with you, do you also seek the priesthood? 11. Surely it is against God that you and all of your company have banded together. For who is Aaron that you should rail against him?"

12. Moses sent for Datan and Aviram, but they said: "We will not come. 13. Is it not enough that you brought us from a land flowing with milk and honey to have us die in the desert, that you would also lord over us? . . . We will not come."

16. Moses said to Korach: "Tomorrow, you and all your followers appear before God, and they and Aaron. 17. Each of you take his fire pan and lay incense on it, and each of you bring his fire pan before God." . . . 19. Then the presence of God appeared to the entire community, 20. and God spoke to Moses and Aaron, saying: 21. "Stand back from this community that I may annihilate them in an instant." 22. But they fell on their faces and said: "O God, Source of the breath of all flesh. When one man sins, will You be angry at the entire community?"

23. God spoke to Moses: 24. "Speak to the community and say: "Withdraw from the abodes of Korach, Datan and Aviram." 25. Moses rose and went to Datan and Aviram, the elders of Israel following him.

26. He addressed the community, saying, "Move away from the tents of these wicked men and do not touch anything that belongs to them, lest you be wiped out for all of their transgressions."

27. So they withdrew from the dwellings of Korach, Datan and Aviram. Now Datan and Aviram had come out and they stood at the entrance of their tents, with their wives, children and little ones. 28. And Moses said: "By this you shall know that it was God who sent me to do all these things. They are not of my own devising. 29. If these men die as all men do, if their lot be the common fate of all mankind, it was not God who sent me. 30. But if God brings about something unheard of, so that the ground opens its mouth and swallows them and their possessions, and they go down alive into Sheol, you shall know that these men have spurned God." 31. No sooner had he finished speaking when 32. the ground under them burst open and the earth swallowed them and their households—all of Korach's people and their belongings. . . . 35. And a fire went forth from God and devoured the two hundred and fifty men.

The Problem

Korach, the great-grandson of Levi, along with Datan, Aviran and On and 250 elected leaders of the Israelite community decide to organize a rebellion against Moses and Aaron. They complain that all the Israelites are holy, and thus there ought not to be a need for Moses and Aaron to raise themselves up above God's congregation. Korach's challenge strikes to the heart of the democratic values so cherished by our Jewish and American traditions: If all the people are created equal, then why should any one person have any authority over another?

Shocked by their accusation, Moses challenges Korach and his followers to bring fire pans and incense with them to the sanctuary the next morning. "God will make known who is holy and who is not," he says.

Turning to Korach, Moses questions his motives. Moses states that Korach had been given special duties in the sanctuary and all kinds of opportunities for leadership. Why, Moses wonders, does Korach also seek the priesthood as well?

Moses then asks Datan and Aviram to meet with him, but they refuse. The next morning Moses and Aaron meet with Korach and his congregation in front of the sanctuary. Each is carrying a firepan with red-hot coals and incense on it. God speaks to Moses and Aaron, telling them to withdraw from Korach and the community because soon they are about to be destroyed. Moses and Aaron then plead to God on behalf of the people: "If one person sins, will You, God, be angry with the entire community?"

God then tells Moses to order the people to withdraw from the area near the tents of Korach, Datan and Aviram. Then, as the people look on, Moses devises the following test and announces to the people: "If these people die a natural death, it will signify that I have not been chosen by God to lead you. However, if they are swallowed by the earth opening up, that will be a sign that God has indeed sent me to lead you." At that point the earth does open up, and Korach, Datan, Aviram and their families, along with 250 followers, perish.

Questions aboud in this story? What were the protests in this story really about? What truly fueled the dispute? What was the real cause of Korach's rebellion? And why the dramatic punishment by earthquake of Korach and his followers? Why does God decide to get involved in this story? Why were innocent children drawn into a rebellion not of their making?

What the Commentaries Say

Rashi: The fact that innocent children are drawn into the rebellion of the Korach story teaches the grievousness of strife, for, while an earthly court does not punish minors, the Heavenly Court makes even suckling infants bear the consequences of their father's sins.

Numbers Rabbah 18:2: This story is a case of family jealousy. Since the priesthood and political leadership had already been taken by Moses and Aaron (sons of Amram, Kohat's oldest son), Korach felt that at least the leadership of the clan should have gone to him, who was the son of Izhar, Kohat's second son. Instead, the appointment had gone to Elizaphan son of Uzziel, who was Kohat's fourth and youngest son.

Hasidic: Korach failed because he wanted to seize greatness and strength for himself with his own hands. Greatness is good only if it is bestowed on a person by Heaven. A person cannot go out and take it for himself.

Ethics of the Fathers 5:17: Every controversy that is in the name of heaven shall in the end lead to a permanent result, but every controversy that is not in the name of heaven shall not lead to a permanent result. Which controversy was in the name of heaven? The controversy of Hillel and Shammai. And which was not in the name of heaven? The controversy of Korach and all his company.

Zohar: Korach quarreled with peace, and one who quarrels with peace quarrels with the Holy Name.

Rabbi Seymour Essrog: There is much personal abuse to which Moses is subjected—facts distorted, accusations heavy with sarcasm intended to provoke and hurt. The biting and taunting words of Korach and his followers have inspired the rabbis to comment *Uvnay Korach lo maytoo*—"the children of Korach have not died—they are still with us." History has been proof to the wisdom of the sages.

Shalom Orzach: Orzach quotes a midrash (Numbers Rabbah 18) in which Korach asks Moses: "A room that is full of holy books, does it require a *mezuzah* on the door?" Korach is saying that since the text of the *mezuzah* is found within the books in the room, there is no need for the *mezuzah*. In the same way, if everybody is already holy, surely they do not need Moses or Aaron. They are as unnecessary as the *mezuzah*. Korach was also trying to say that since the Jewish people were already good and holy, then they could sit back and relax. Everything was fine. They did not need Moses to lead them anywhere, and they did not need to change anything at all. Orzach thus argues that the lesson of the Korach episode is as follows: Korach's arguments were first and foremost an attempt to get rid of Moses. On a more serious level, Korach wanted to suggest that once goodness and holiness had been given to the Jewish people, there is no need to do anything further. Korach challenged the function of *mitzvot* and to a great extent our very essence.

Nachmanides: He notes that Korach organizes his protest when the spies return from the Land of Israel with their troubling negative report. This report causes the Israelites to complain and grumble about the difficult life they had in the desert. Korach, Nachmanides asserts, finds the opportune time to pick his quarrel with Moses, assuming that the people will side with him because they are so frustrated with their own situation.

Nechama Leibowitz: She posits that Korach and his followers were simply a band of malcontents, each harboring personal grievances against authority, animated by individual pride and ambition. In her estimation, they deserve their punishment because all of their motives were self-serving, aimed at dividing the Jewish people.

Shlomo Riskin: The conflict between Moses and Korach reflects a tug of war within the human spirit. Korach denies the importance of the laws. He says, "Who needs the system of do's an don't, you shalls and you shall nots? We are already holy." Certainly this perspective was attractive to every Israelite who wanted to be left alone. Who wants to be told what to do and what not to do? If I want to commit adultery, who are you to tell me I shouldn't?

Questions

1. According to commentator Pinchas Peli, each wondrous event in the Bible is meant to call our attention to an important lesson. What do you think is the lesson taught by the miraculous destruction of Korach and his followers by an earthquake?

2. Is there any difference between the rebellion of Korach and that of Datan and Aviram? Are there modern parallels to their protests?

3. What is your opinion of the severe punishment of Korach and his followers? Does the punishment fit the crime? What is the crime?

4. Korach claims that Moses and Aaron are acting as if they are more holy than others. Can you think of any modern-day examples of similar accusations?

5. Ethics of the Fathers states that there are two kinds of disputes: one that is pursued for a "heavenly" or good cause and one that is pursued for selfish reasons. Give examples of arguments for the sake of heaven and those not for the sake of heaven.

6. The Bible story states that "all the congregation is holy." (Numbers 16:3) Who is the congregation?

7. In the Bible story Moses makes this plea: "Shall one man sin and will You, God, be angry with the entire congregation?" If you were God, how would you respond to Moses' question? Why do you think God responded to it in the way that God did in this story?

8. Why should the Israelites merit instant destruction if they happened to be standing among Korach's band? Surely Aaron, who was with them, was unharmed when the ground opened underneath them. What was the purpose of the divine demand for the Israelites to separate themselves from Korach?

9. How do you understand the issue of the wondrous phenomenon of the earthquake to punish Korach? Does God, or can God, interrupt the normal cycle of nature to reward or to punish? Should God wish to punish someone for a grievous sin, can God cause the earth to open and swallow alive an individual in order to punish?

10. What are you, impressions of the leadership skills of both Moses and Aaron vis-à-vis the rebellion of Korach? Do you think that they handled the situation well? Are there things that perhaps they should have done that they did not do? What do you think you might have done if you found yourself in a situation where someone challenged your authority?

11. It has been said by several commentators that Korach was a master of words, and that is why he was so very dangerous. He misused words and knew how to chain people with words. Do you agree that Korach used words manipulatively? Can you cite some examples?

IX. The Red Heifer
The mystery of the holy cow

The Bible Story (Numbers 19:1–13)

1. God said to Moses and Aaron: 2. This is the law that God has commanded: Tell the people of Israel to bring you a red cow without blemish, in which there is no defect and on which no yoke has been laid. 3. Give it to Eleazar the priest. It shall be taken outside the camp and slaughtered in his presence. 4. Eleazar the priest shall take some of its blood with his finger and sprinkle it seven times toward the front of the Tent of Meeting. 5. The cow shall be burned in his sight—its hide, flesh, and blood shall be burned, its dung also. 6. The priest shall take cedar wood, hyssop, and crimson stuff, and throw them into the fire consuming the cow. 7. The priest shall wash his clothes and bathe his body in water. Following that the priest shall reenter the camp but he shall be unclean until evening. 8. He who performs the burning shall also wash his clothing in water, bathe his body and be unclean until evening. 9. A man who is clean shall gather up the ashes of the cow and deposit them outside the camp in a clean place, to be kept for water of purification for the

Israelite community. It is for cleansing. 10. One who gathers up the ashes of the cow shall also wash his clothes and be unclean until evening. . . .

11. One who touches the corpse of any human being shall be unclean for seven days. 12. He shall cleanse himself with it on the third day and on the seventh day, and then be clean; if he should fail to clean himself on the third and seventh days, he shall not be clean. 13. Whoever touches a corpse, the body of a person who has died, and does not cleanse himself defiles God's tabernacle. That person shall be cut off from Israel.

The Problem

The rules regarding the red heifer are among the most mysterious laws in all of the Torah. They prescribe a process of purification for anyone who has come into contact with a dead body. This is accomplished through sprinkling a person with the ashes of an unblemished red heifer. Most difficult of all of the aspects of this rite is that the sprinkling has a cleansing effect, but those who handle the ashes are unclean until nightfall.

A midrash (Tanchuma Hukkat 26) relates that a gentile once came to Rabbi Yochanan ben Zakkai and asked about the reason for the ritual. The rabbi gave him a rational answer but later admitted to his students that a mystery was involved, for in and of themselves the dead were not impure nor the ashes purifying. "But, said the sage," this is what God has decreed, and you may not violate God's law." The puzzlement over the contradiction has persisted to this day, and we may well speculate whether this rite of ancient origin does not reflect the inherent and thus persistent contradiction between life and death. They are eternally linked in tension, and whoever touches them incurs both purity and impurity at the same time

What the Commentaries Say

Joseph Bechor Shor: He explains that the ritual of the red heifer is meant to prevent Jews from sinning by contact with corpses. It is a natural tendency to cling to loved ones who have died and occasionally, to want to caress and embrace their dead bodies, if only for the final time. Shor posits that to warn Jews against the practice in some societies of worshiping the dead or wearing garments made from their skin or bones, the Torah declares contact with a dead body defiling.

Nechama Leibowitz: ". . . the priest shall take cedar wood, hyssop and crimson stuff, and throw them into the fire consuming the cow." (Numbers 19:6) She posits that a sprinkling by water mixed with ashes from the red cow is the only rite for purification from such sin. The ritual possesses both educational and purifying powers. It not only purifies from sin, but it also functions as a dramatic reminder that Jews are forbidden to touch or admire the bodies of their dead.

Dr. Robert Kunin: ". . . the priest shall take cedar wood, hyssop, and crimson stuff, and throw them into the fire consuming the cow." (Numbers 19:6) Analyzing the ritual of the red cow, research chemist Dr. Robert Kunin writes that our biblical ancestors were most aware of water pollution as well as the technology for treating it. A chemist analyzing the ritual of the red heifer must conclude that the mixture of ashes is a mixture of granular and powdered activated carbon and bone char—a mixture of virgin carbonaceous adsorbents capable of removing practically all known toxins, viruses, and pollutants, including radioactivity. Kunin notes that the components of the ash and the basic method of treating water as described in Numbers is essentially the only method currently approved by the United States government.

Sforno: ". . . the priest shall take cedar wood, hyssop and crimson stuff, and throw them into the fire consuming the cow." (Numbers 19:6) Sforno offers a symbolic explanation of the rite of the red heifer. He points out that the priest takes cedar wood, identified with pride because the cedar stands tall, and hyssop, identified with humility because it is a fragrant low-growing plant, along with red scarlet thread, identified with sinfulness, and places all three into the fire consuming the red heifer. The ashes, which combine pride, humility and sinfulness, are then mixed with water for the purification ritual.

For Sforno, the power associated with the red cow pulls the transgressor back from the evil of pride toward the ideal of humility. The mixture of ashes and water provides a method for repentance. Specifically, if arrogance pushes one to neglect the laws of Torah by touching a corpse, that one then requires purification. The ritual for this purpose is composed of symbolic messages. By being sprinkled with the mixture of ashes from the red cow, cedar wood, hyssop and a scarlet thread, the sinner who has allowed pride to rule is purified and reminded to pursue humility and more moderate paths of behavior.

Philo: ". . . the priest shall take cedar wood, hyssop and crimson stuff, and throw them into the fire consuming the cow." (Numbers 19:6) The mixture of water and ashes reminds men of what elements they consist, for knowledge of oneself is the most wholesome form of purification.

Hinnuch: He professes that he never hesitated to rationalize the *mitzvot* because he felt that youth was eager to ask questions which must be answered with valid reasons. However, in the case of the red heifer, he admits to the total absence of human logic and makes no comment.

Abarbanel: "He that touches a dead body shall be declared unclean for seven days." (Numbers 19:11) Man stands on the highest rung of the ladder of the animal kingdom. His body is purer and his intelligence is superior to that of any other creature. When he dies, he decomposes more rapidly than any other animal. He lives and dies in a distinct class by himself. By coming in contact with corpses, thereby rendering himself unclean, he mars his superior image by not showing appreciation for the superiority which God granted him. The Torah instructed that the person who touched a corpse should be sprinkled with the ashes of a red heifer in order to emphasize that such a person commits a heinous sin and should have been destroyed as the red heifer was. He was guilty of not living up to the high standard expected of him.

In this ritual a cedar and a hyssop are included because great Jews are compared to tall cedars and ordinary Jews to the lowly hyssop. The entire ritual is aimed at both of these categories in equal measure.

Targum Yerushalmi: Bamidbar Rabbah, chapter 2: The slaying of the red heifer was an expiatory rite to atone for the sin of having worshiped the golden calf. The red heifer makes atonement for the idolatry of the golden calf.

Questions

1. There are commentators who posit that religion and ritual are matters of faith and should not be subject to reason. Do you agree with such commentators? Is it important to know the rationale behind a certain ritual in order to gain maximum benefit when doing it?

2. On what Shabbat and preceding what Jewish holiday is the story of the red heifer always read? What is the origin of this custom?

3. Several commentators have suggested symbolic meanings for the ritual of the red heifer. Which carries the most meaning for you?

4. The famed Rabbi Yochanan ben Zakkai, head of the Sanhedrin at the time of the destruction of the Temple, was once asked by a non-Jew to explain the ritual of the red heifer. "Do you really believe that some ashes from a red cow purify a person who has touched a corpse? Are you not practicing magic?" he challenged. How would you answer this question?

5. Can you think of any other mitzvot in the Torah that appear to you to be irrational? What are they?

6. The red heifer mixture was able to purify the impure and render impure at the same time those preparing the mixture. Can you think of some modern-day examples of something that purifies the impure and yet at the same time has within it the power to render the pure impure?

X. Striking the Rock
A story of trust

The Bible Story (Numbers 20:2–13)

2. The community was without water, and they joined against Moses and Aaron. 3. The people argued with Moses saying, "If only we had died when our brothers perished at the instance of God. 4. Why have you brought God's congregation into this wilderness for us and for our beasts to die there? 5. Why did you make us leave Egypt to bring us to this wretched place, a place with no grain or figs or vines or pomegranates? There is not even water to drink." 6. Moses and Aaron came away from the congregation to the entrance of the Tent of Meeting, and fell on their faces. The Presence of God appeared to them, and 7. God spoke to Moses saying: 8. "You and your brother Aaron, take the rod and assemble the community, and before their very eyes order the rock to yield its water.

"Thus you shall produce water for them from the rock and provide drink for the congregation and their beasts." 9. Moses took the rod from before God, as God had commanded him. 10. Moses and Aaron assembled the congregation in front of the rock, and he said to them:

"Listen, you rebels, shall we get water for you out of this rock?" 11. And Moses raised his hand and struck the rock twice with his rod. Out came abundant water, and the community and their animals drank.

12. But God said to Moses and Aaron: "Because you did not trust Me enough to affirm My sanctity in the sight of the Israelites, therefore you shall not lead this congregation into the land that I have given them." 13. Those are the Waters of Merivah—meaning that the Israelites quarrelled with God—through which God affirmed His sanctity.

The Problem

This Bible story is the second murmuring to take place at Merivah, the first taking place in Exodus 17:1–7. In both instances water is miraculously provided from a rock. We are told in this story that Moses and Aaron will not lead the Israelites into the Promised Land. Many commentators see the transgression of Moses and Aaron related to their lack of trust in God. They were to have ordered the rock to yield water, but Moses instead struck the rock twice with his rod. How could such a seemingly minor transgression on the part of Moses and Aaron wipe out a lifetime of merit and service to the Israelite community? Does the punishment of Moses and Aaron really fit the crime? If Moses, who held the staff and spoke to the Israelites, did something wrong, why is Aaron also punished? What kind of a God would do this to two great leaders? How can a God of justice inflict such a sentence upon loyal leaders?

What the Commentaries Say

Numbers Rabbah 19:10: "You and your brother Aaron, take the rod and assemble the community, and before their very eyes order the rock to yield its water." (Numbers 20:8) Both Moses and Aaron are guilty of arrogance. Their instruction is to **speak** to the rock, not **strike** it. Instead, Moses publicly strikes it not once, but twice! In doing so, Moses implies a lack of faith in God to bring forth water.

Moses Maimonides: "Listen, you rebels, shall we get water for you out of this rock?" (Numbers 20:10) He claims that God punishes Moses because of his exasperation with the complaints and quarreling of the Israelites. Extreme anger is his downfall. Intelligence and impatience condemn him. Moses flies into a rage. He insults the people by calling them "rebels." And in doing so, he fails as a leader and as a model for their own behavior.

Samson Raphael Hirsch: "Listen, you rebels, shall we get water for you out of this rock?" (Numbers 20:10) He explains that the sin of Moses grew out of his deep disappointment with the people. He is stunned that after forty years he must still carry his staff to prove his credibility. For that reason, he speaks in words of deep reproach, and in passionate agitation struck the rock. It was, Hirsch insists, the impulsive vehement raising of the rod in which the wrong of Moses consisted.

Pinchus Peli: He asserts that Aaron is condemned because he watches silently while his brother Moses is out of control. He does nothing to pacify him nor does he speak out to defend the Israelites. Through his not protesting, he becomes an accomplice to Moses' crime.

Nachmanides: "Listen, you rebels, shall we get water for you out of this rock?" (Numbers 20:10) He points out that it is not Aaron and Moses who are angry, but rather the people's anger leads to their complaints. As for Moses and Aaron, Nachmanides posits that their sin lies in misleading the Israelites. They speak carelessly to the people. Gathering them before the rock, they declare: "Listen, rebels, shall **we** get water for you out of this rock?" rather than "shall **God** get water for you out of this rock?" Their words imply that it is their power, not God's, that will cause water to come forth. This deliberate deception of the people, argues Nachmanides, is the serious wrongdoing of Moses and Aaron.

Levi Isaac of Berdichev: "Listen, you rebels, shall we get water for you out of this rock?" (Numbers 19:10) He maintains that Moses and Aaron are punished for how they express their criticism of the people. They criticize with very harsh words. They shame the Israelites by calling them "rebels." It is thus their lack of support for their people that brings about their punishment.

Morris Adler: He asserts that the Torah intentionally does not spell out the real sin of Moses and Aaron. In this way the Torah teaches by indirection that the sins of Moses and Aaron are not necessarily overt and obvious, but likely subtle and yet still destructive.

Questions

1. Which of the many sins suggested by the commentators makes the most sense? Why?

2. Some modern commentators have stated that Moses was entrapped. After all, God told him to take his staff along, so that's why he hit the rock. What is your opinion about Moses' possible entrapment?

3. What, in your opinion, was the sin of Moses? Was it fair that he should be so utterly condemned?

4. In the story in Exodus 17:5–7, Moses is commanded to strike the rock and water will issue from it. If Moses was told once before to obtain water out of the rock by striking it, how could he not but strike again when asked to repeat the miracle?

5. The story of Moses hitting the rock is alluded to in one of the opening psalms of the Kabbalat Shabbat Friday evening service. Which psalm is it, and why do you think this story is to be remembered on Friday evening of Shabbat?

XI. Balaam and the Talking Donkey

Can a non-Jew be a prophet?

The Bible Story (Selected verses from Numbers 22–24)

Chapter 22

4. Balak son of Zippor, king of Moab, 5. sent messengers to Balaam son of Beor to invite him, saying, "There is a people that came out of Egypt. It hides the earth from view, and it is settled next to me. 6. Come and put a curse upon this people for me, since they are too numerous for me. . . . For I know that he whom you bless is blessed, and he whom you curse is cursed." . . .

9. God came to Balaam and said, "What do these people want of you?" 10. Balaam said to God, "Balak sent me this message:

11. 'Here is a people that came out from Egypt and hides the earth from view. Come now and curse them for me.'" . . . 12. But God said to Balaam, "Do not go with them. You must not curse that people, for they are blessed."

13. Balaam arose in the morning and said to Balak's dig-

nitaries, "Go back to your own country, for God will not let me go with you." 14. The Moabite dignitaries left, and they came to Balak and said, "Balak refused to come with us."

15. Then Balak sent other dignitaries, more numerous and distinguished than the first. 16. They came to Balaam and said to him: "Thus says Balak. Please do not refuse to come.

17. I will richly reward you and I will do anything that you ask of me. Only come and curse this people." 18. Balaam replied to Balak's officials, "Though Balak were to give me his house full of silver and gold, I could not do anything contrary to the command of God." . . . 20. That night God came to Balaam and said to him, "If these men have come to invite you, you may go with them. But whatever I command you, that you shall do."

21. When he arose in the morning, Balaam saddled his donkey and departed with the Moabite dignitaries. 22. But God was angry at his going, so an angel of God placed himself in the way as an adversary. He was riding on the donkey, with his two servants alongside. 23. When the donkey noticed the angel of God standing in the way, with his sword drawn in his hand, the donkey swerved from the road and went into the fields, and Balaam beat the donkey to turn her back onto the road. 24. The angel of God then stationed himself in a lane between the vineyards. 25. The donkey, seeing the angel of God, pressed herself against the wall and squeezed Balaam's foot against the wall. So he beat her again. 26. Once more the angel of God moved forward and stationed himself on a spot so narrow that there was no room to swerve right or left. 27. When the donkey now saw the

angel of God, she lay down under Balaam, and Balaam was furious and beat her with a stick.

28. Then God opened the donkey's mouth and she said to Balaam, "What have I done to you that you have beaten me these three times?" 29. Balaam said to the donkey, "You have made a mockery of me. If I had a sword with me, I'd kill you." 30. The donkey said to Balaam, "I am the donkey that you have been riding all along until this day. Have I been in the habit of doing thus to you?" And he answered: "No." 31. Then God uncovered Balaam's eyes and he saw the angel of God standing in the way, his drawn sword in his hand. 32.The angel of God said to him, "Why have you beaten your donkey three times? It is I who came out as an adversary, for the errand is obnoxious to me. 33. And when the donkey saw me, she shied away from me those three times." . . . 34. Balaam said to the angel: "I erred because I did not know that you were standing in my way. If you still disapprove, I will turn back." 35. But the angel of God said to Balaam,"Go with the men. But you must say nothing except that which I tell you." So Balaam went on with the dignitaries.

Chapter 23

4. God manifested Himself to Balaam and 5. put a word in his mouth, saying, "Return to Balak and speak thus." 6. He went to him and found him standing beside his offerings, and the Moabite dignitaries with him. 17. Balak asked: "What did God say?" 18. And he took up his theme and said:

19. " . . . God is not man to be capricious, or mortal to change God's mind.

"Would God speak and not act, promise and not fulfill?

20. "My message was to bless: When God blesses, I cannot reverse it." . . .

25. Thereupon Balak said to Balaam: "Don't curse them and don't bless them." 26. In reply, Balaam said to Balak: "But I told you: Whatever God says, I must do."

Chapter 24

1. Now Balaam, seeing that it pleased God to bless Israel, did not, as on previous occasions, go in search of omens, but turned his face toward the wilderness. 2. As Balaam looked up and saw Israel encamped tribe by tribe, the spirit of God came upon him. 3. Taking up his theme he said:

"Word of Balaam son of Beor, Word of the man whose eye is true.

4. "Word of him who hears God's speech, who beholds visions from the Almighty, prostrate, but with eyes unveiled:

5. "How goodly are your tents, O Jacob, your dwellings, O Israel." . . .

10. Enraged at Balaam, Balak struck his hands together. "I called you," Balak said to Balaam, "to curse my enemies, and instead you have blessed them these three times.

11. "Go back to your own place. I was going to reward you richly, but God has denied you the reward." 12. Balaam replied to Balak, "But I even told the messengers you sent to me. 13. 'Though Balak were to give me his house full of sil-

ver and gold, I could not of my own accord do anything good or bad contrary to God's command. What God says, that I must do.' 14. And now, as I go back to my people, let me inform you of what this people will do to your people in days to come. . . ."

25. Then Balaam set out on his journey back home, and Balak also went his way.

The Problem

The tale of Balak and Balaam is one of the most intriguing and unusual in all of the Torah. Balak, king of Moab, fears that the Israelites will attack his country. He then decides to send Balaam, known as a pagan prophet, with special powers to bless and curse. Balak promises to reward Balaam for cursing the people of Israel, and Balaam takes some time to consider the offer. During the night God tells Balaam that he must not curse the Israelites, for they are a people that are blessed. Later on in the story God tells Balaam to go with the messengers, but to say only what God commands.

Balaam set out for Moab on his donkey. At this point, the most macabre dialogue in the Torah ensues. God opens the mouth of the donkey and she says to Balaam: "What have I done to you that you have beaten me three times?" Finally God opens Balaam's eyes and he sees the angel of God standing in front of him with a drawn sword. The angel scolds Balaam for hitting his donkey, and Balaam, realizing how God opposes his mission to curse the Israelites, tries to pacify him. Finally the angel permits Balaam to resume his journey with the one proviso that he say only that which God tells him.

Instead of damning the Israelites, Balaam blesses them, promising that the Israelites will triumph over all of their enemies, including the people of Moab.

Interestingly, the Talmud (Baba Batra 15a) calls this Bible story "The Book of Balaam." The story raises a number of questions and problems. Who is Balaam? What are his powers? Is he an enemy or a friend of the Jewish people? Does God really speak to him and appear to his donkey? How significant are these events in which Moses is not even mentioned and in which the main characters are non-Jews? Is Balaam a prophet?

What the Commentaries Say

Ibn Ezra: He claims that Balaam is a deceptive schemer, a dangerous man. He substantiates his accusation by pointing out that Balaam never tells Balak's messengers that God will not permit him to curse the Israelites. He allows them to believe that he is willing to damn the king's enemies. Moreover, Balaam orders Balak to build altars and make sacrifices without telling Balak that God will permit him only to bless the Israelites. Balaam withholds information and distorts the truth. He seeks to take advantage of the king's fears for his own financial gain.

Gunther Plaut: He quotes the biblical scholar W.F. Albright, who concludes that Balaam was really a North-Syrian diviner from the Euphrates valley, and that he became a convert to Israel's faith in God. Later he abandoned Israel and joined the Midianites in their fight against the Israelites.

Nechama Leibowitz: She posits that Balaam is a prophet, not a sorcerer or diviner for hire. She applauds Balaam's spiritual growth in the Bible story from a man who sees less than his own donkey to a person who achieves pure prophecy.

Martin Buber: Disagreeing with Leibowitz, Buber asserts that Balaam is not commissioned nor sent by God. He fails to make decisions on his own. Rather, God makes decisions for him. Although Balaam may have the potential to be a prophet and take initiative, he never fulfills that potential. He remains aloof from others, and never engages others. Instead, he announces God's words, exercising no will of his own. He speaks about tomorrow but does not participate in making the choices and decisions that will shape the future. Consequently, he remains a common magician.

Robert Alter: He claims that the entire Balaam story is meant to demonstrate the flaws of paganism. Paganism, with its notion that divine power can be manipulated by a caste of professionals through a set of carefully prescribed procedures, is trapped in the reflexes of a mechanistic world-view, while from the biblical perspective, reality is in fact controlled by the will of an omnipotent God beyond all human manipulation. For the pagan, knowledge of the world and how to dominate it is consigned to expert magicians or seers like Balaam. That explains why Balak is willing to pay him such a high price to curse Israel. By contrast, the Torah puts forth the view that no human can truly comprehend, and certainly not manipulate, God's will. God's will is beyond understanding, too awesome to be grasped.

Maimonides: "Then God opened the donkey's mouth and she spoke to Balaam." (Numbers 22:28) He postulates that Balaam experienced the episode of the talking donkey as a vision.

Me'am Lo'ez: Balaam did not have it in his power either to bless or curse. The blessing was redundant—God had already blessed, and the curse ineffective. Why then did God prevent him from cursing? Because he foresaw Israel's future sins and punishments. He did not want the nations to say: "It was Balaam's curse which caused it."

S.R. Hirsch: Balaam wants to correct God's plan for the world and is blinder than his own beast. He wants to overcome God's resistance but must yield to his animal. He wants to spoil a whole people with his word, and his anger is helpless before the donkey. He wants to prance before the great and becomes a laughing stock before his servants.

Joseph ibn Kaspi: The curse of Balaam had no objective potency either in terms of the author or the deed. Its effect must only be considered from the point of view of those at the receiving end, namely the Israelites. Balaam was a renowned sorcerer, and people were impressed both then and now by sorcerers and diviners. There is no point in asking the reason for the belief of Balak and his company, just as there is no reason for doing so in the case of Jacob and Esau, who attached such importance to their father's blessing. If they did, how much more so the Israelites of those days, in particular the women and children, who would be greatly affected by the maledictions of such a renowned sorcerer.

A true friend will save his colleague any pain, even if he knows that no danger will ensue. Similarly, the Almighty, out of the abundance of His love for Israel, prevented Balaam from cursing them, though God was aware that his curses were impotent. But God did not rest content with this. He went so far as to make Balaam bless the people to give them pleasure.

Abarbanel: "I beg you, curse these people, for they are too strong for me." (Numbers 22:6) He claimed that Balaam's sorcery was world-famous. Balak referred to his renown when he said: "For I know that he whom you bless is blessed, and he whom you curse is cursed." Had Balaam cursed Israel, the surrounding nations would have plucked up courage and gone to do battle with Israel on the strength of the curses. But when they learned how God had turned them into blessings, they would then realize who was Master and would lose all desire to fight His people.

Questions

1. Nechama Leibowitz once wrote that Balaam may have begun with sinister intentions toward Israel, but evolves into a person whose faith in God increases with experience. He ascends from a common sorcerer to a prophet who hears the word of God. What do you think of Leibowitz's assertion? Do you think Balaam is a true prophet?

2. In what ways does Balaam differ from a Moses or a Jeremiah?

3. Can you identify any Balaam-type people in contemporary society? Describe them.

4. The last blessing that Balaam offers is: "How goodly are your tents, O Jacob, your dwelling places, O Israel." (In Hebrew, *ma tovu ohalecha ya'akove meeshkenotecha yisrael.*) Do you recognize these words from the prayerbook? If so, in which prayer do you find them? Why do you think that these words were chosen for inclusion in the prayerbook? How do you feel about a pagan's words used as a Jewish prayer.

5. The Talmud (Baba Batra 60a) provides an additional reason for Balaam's inability to curse Israel. Balaam looked up and saw Israel encamped "tribe by tribe" (Numbers 24:2) He saw that the tribes were set apart from each other and that the tent openings did not face each other. No one could see into the tent of anyone else. This became the source for

the ruling that one may not build a door directly opposite the door of a neighbor, or make a window in line with a neighbor's window. This insures privacy and respect of personal dignity and is in keeping with the value of modesty in behavior. Why might this Israelite practice deter Balaam from cursing the Israelites? How is privacy assured for each family in your house?

6. Some rabbinic commentators have placed Balaam in the same category as a Haman or an Amalek. Others call him prophet on a par with Moses. How do you explain these two different views? Is there evidence of both evil and good in Balaam?

7. Rabbi Dan Shevitz has some interesting assertions related to the story of Balaam and Balak. He writes that the more we are drawn into this story, the more questions confront us. Why spend three whole chapters of the Bible with the Moabites? What do we care if a pagan prophet listens or does not listen to his employer's instructions? Why have we left Israel in the middle of her journeys? Where is Moses in the story? Rabbi Shevitz also notes that Moses and Balaam are never seen together. When Moses leaves, Balaam arrives. When Balaam departs for Mesopotamia at the end of his mission, Moses reappears. In short, Rabbi Shevitz hypothesizes that Moses and Balaam are the same person. What is your opinion of this theory? Can you find any traces of a resemblance in the Bible story between Moses and Balaam?

8. Why do you think that God needed to prevent Balaam from cursing the Israelites? Why should they have cared about his curse?

9. According to the Sifrei, "There has never arisen a prophet in Israel like Moses, but in the gentile world there has arisen. And who? Balaam the son of Beor." What is your opinion of the Sifrei? Why is Balaam so special?

XII. Pinchas the Zealot
The danger of fanaticism

The Bible Story (Numbers 25:6–13)

6. Just then one of the Israelites came and brought a Midianite woman over to his companions, in the sight of Moses and the whole community of Israel, who were crying at the entrance of the Tent of Meeting. 7. When Pinchas, son of Eleazar son of Aaron the Priest, saw this, he left the assembly and taking a spear in his hand, 8. he followed the Israelite into the chamber and stabbed both of them, the Israelite and the woman through the belly. Then the plague against the Israelites was checked. 9. Those who died of the plague numbered twenty-four thousand.

10. God spoke to Moses saying: 11. "Pinchas, son of Eleazar son of Aaron the priest, has turned back My anger from the Israelites by displaying among them his passion for Me, so that I did not wipe out the Israelite people in My passion.

12. "Say therefore, 'I grant him My pact of friendship. 13. It shall be for him and his descendants after him a pact of priesthood for all time, because he took zealous action for his God, thus making expiation for the Israelites."

The Problem

According to the Torah, Midianite women are leading the Israelites into harlotry and idolatry. In this Bible story, Pinchas, the son of Eleazar, kills a Midianite woman and Zimri, who have entered a tent to have sex. Pinchas' zealousness saves the Israelites from a plague, and God rewards him with a covenant of peace and his descendants with the office of the priesthood for all time.

The incident of Pinchas's spearing and killing Zimri, a tribal head of the Israelites, raises serious moral questions. Did Pinchas do the right thing? Should he be praised or condemned for his zeal, rewarded or punished for killing Zimri and Cosbi? Since Pinchas seems to benefit from breaking the commandment "You shall not murder," how does one explain the apparent contradiction?

Early rabbinic tradition is divided on whether the act of Pinchas is justified. Some say that Pinchas rushes to execute justice without consulting Moses, the highest leader in the community. Rav finds fault with Pinchas' fanaticism, arguing that although Pinchas may have acted within the law, he should have allowed God to execute its provisions rather than doing it himself.

On the other hand, Samuel praises Pinchas for his zeal, claiming that the case in this Bible story is one in which God's law is being publicly desecrated, and therefore Pinchas is correct for his decision.

What the Commentaries Say

Maimonides: "And he took a spear in his hand and followed the Israelite into the chamber and speared both of them." (Numbers 25:7) He asserts that a Jew may be put to death by zealots if he is found having sexual intercourse with a non-Jewish woman or harlot. He points to the example of Pinchas, stating that zealots are justified in killing such a person only if they catch him during the act itself. Should they kill him afterwards, however, they are to be charged with murder.

Jerusalem Talmud, Sanhedrin 9:7: While Pinchas did the right thing by taking the law into his own hand, he erred in the way in which he acted. He should have consulted with Moses, and perhaps others. His actions would have been more just if he gained the community's consent rather than acting alone.

Alshech: "Pinchas followed the Israelite into the chamber and stabbed both of them, the Israelite and the woman through the belly." (Numbers 25:8) He suggests that Pinchas' zeal may not have originated in the pure motive of defending the ethical laws of Torah. Rather, his stabbing of Zimri and Cosbi is a deliberate act meant to prove he is worthy of the priesthood and of passing on that privilege to his descendants. Alshech believes that Pinchas has an ulterior motive for his demonstration of zeal. He rushes forward to punish Zimri and Cozbi, not out of a sense of outrage at their public

insult to God and Torah, but because he wishes to attract
Moses' attention and secure the office of the priesthood for
himself and his offspring. His act, therefore, must be
denounced.

S.R. Hirsch: "I grant him my pact of friendship."
(Numbers 25:12) He justifies and praises Pinchas' act as not
merely an external forward rush but the result of his deep
inner feeling that made a betrayal of God's affairs feel like a
treachery against one's own self. Zimri, he explains, is not an
ordinary Israelite. He ranks as a prince, as one who should
set the example as a pattern of noble moral purity for his people. His public act of entering a tent with the intention of
having sex with a Midianite woman derided God. It debased
the Jewish people and faith.

In the face of Zimri's disgraceful public behavior, someone is needed to restore the people's faith in God and to
demonstrate Israel's commitment to God's commandments.
Pinchas, asserts Hirsch, understands this, and believes that
unless he acts, the people will forfeit their relationship with
God. Pinchas' actions were an act of bravery, and for this reason God rewards him with a covenant of friendship and that
his descendants will forever be designated as priests.

Naphtali Tzvi Judah Berlin: "I grant him my pact of
friendship." (Numbers 25:12) He suggests that while
Pinchas' zeal may reflect deep conviction, it also reveals dia-
bolic and corrupt motives. People who are prepared to murder and terrorize others, and destroy for a cause are often

filled with hatred and the poison of prejudice. As a result their acts of vengeance against others are often followed by self-destructive acts. Berlin posits that Pinchas, despite his demonstration of commitment to God's Torah, is deeply disturbed by his zealous behavior and for taking the law into his own hands.

According to Berlin, God gives Pinchas the "covenant of friendship" not as a reward for his impulsive behavior but a cure for it. The covenant is meant to calm him.

Samuel B. Press: "I grant him my pact of friendship." (Numbers 25:12) He points out the when the Torah speaks of the covenant of peace that God gave to Pinchas, the word *shalom* is written with a defective letter. The letter *vav* is not complete. Thus something is lacking in the "peace" achieved by Pinchas. We are reminded that we cannot allow the **means** to justify the **ends**. Pinchas is an exception, an anomaly in Jewish life. We need other standards.

Irwin Groner: " . . . because he (Pinchas) took zealous action for his God." (Numbers 25:13) Pinchas and his violent act seem to be in conflict with today's moral standards. One aspect of the story bears careful attention: the character of the priest. It is not so much the act as the motivation of Pinchas which evokes the praise of the Bible. Pinchas was filled with *kinah* or "zeal." The word "zeal" is derived from the Greek term meaning "to boil." The zealous person boils inwardly, filled with passion for a cause. The opposite of zeal is coldness and indifference.

Like any other great force, zeal can be dangerous. In excess it can be destructive, generating a fanaticism that is cruel and bitter.

Baruch Epstein: The deed of Pinchas must be animated by a genuine, unadulterated spirit of zeal to advance the glory of God. In this case, who can tell whether the perpetrator is not really prompted by some selfish motive, maintaining that he is doing it for the sake of God, when he has actually committed murder? That was why the sages wished to excommunicate Pinchas, had not the Holy Spirit testified that his zeal for God was genuine.

Mendenhall: "The plague that struck the Israelites stopped. In that plague, 24,000 people died." (Numbers 25:8–9) He posits that it is likely that the plague in the Bible story was the result of their contact with the Midianites. Zimri boldly followed a pagan precedent for dealing with such a mysterious affliction. And by his public act he urged his fellow Israelites to engage in prostitution as a means of warding off the plague. The result was that the disease spread more rapidly. Pinchas did not act out of superior medical knowledge. Rather, he saw in Zimri's act an open breach of the covenant. There was no precedent in the brief history of the people to determine how to deal with such a religious and moral emergency. Mendenhall makes it appear plausible that this was the first incident in which God's power over life and death (in a juridical sense) passed to the people. Pinchas' impulsive deed was not merely a kind of battlefield execution but reflected his apprehension that the demands of God needed human realization and required a dramatic example against permissiveness in the religious realm. The Torah, by obviously approving strongly, implies that this was the proper way to halt further religious disintegration and to repair the breach of the covenant.

Hatam Sofer: " . . . displaying among them his passion for for Me, so that I did not wipe out the Israelite people in My passion." (Numbers 25:11) "While he was zealous for My sake among them, I did not consume the Children of Israel." In other words, all the Jews were really zealous at the blatant sin of Zimri, but they lacked the courage to carry out what they felt needed to be done. Pinchas thus did what everyone else thought, and that was why "I did not consume the Children of Israel."

Questions

1. Why would God mandate the death of all the leaders, innocent and guilty alike?

2. Were Pinchas' actions legal, or not?

3. Why did God give Pinchas a "covenant of peace" for slaying Cozbi and Zimri? Why would God reward Pinchas for a violent and impulsive act of killing?

4. Why did Moses not respond? Alternatively, why did he not challenge God?

5. How do you feel about Pinchas' actions? Should he be praised for his zeal?

6. Are there times when one should take the law into his/her own hands in the face of public lethargy? If yes, when? If no, why not?

7. What is the major critical problem of the entire Baal-Peor incident? (Hint: Compare God's solution of the crisis to that of Moses.)

8. The Hebrew word *kinah* (zeal) appears more than 80 times in the Bible. Here are some places in which it occurs. Look up the following verses and see what *kinah* means in each of them:
Deuteronomy 29:19; Job 5:2; II Kings 19:31; Numbers 11:29; Proverbs 14:11; I Kings 19:10, 14.

9. According to Rabbi Gunther Plaut (*A Modern Torah Commentary*), Pinchas saw in Zimri's act an open breach of the covenant. Pinchas' impulsive deed was not merely a kind of battlefield execution but reflected his apprehension that the demands of God needed human realization and required a memorable and dramatic example against permissiveness in the religious realm. How is this view expressed by current religious zealots?

10. Several years ago a Brooklyn-born Israeli settler named Baruch Goldstein entered the Cave of Machpelah, a shrine holy to both Jews and Arabs, and proceeded to gun down 30 Moslem worshipers. Some say that a feeling of powerlessness gripped Baruch Goldstein as he watched the negotiations for peace unfold which ultimately affected his life. Have you ever felt powerless? How did it feel? Did you ever react to your state of powerlessness in a justified way?

11. Do we need fanatics to stand for principles and for behaviors which most of us are not able to live up to? Would we have most of the basic institutions and values we consider sacred if not for the fanatics of our history? Can we hold tightly to what we believe in without offending or harming other people?

List of Commentators

Early Commentators

Abarbanel, Don Isaac. Fifteenth-century Spanish commentator.

Alshech, Moshe ben Chayim: Sixteenth-century commentator who lived in Safed.

Arama, Isaac. Author of the Torah commentary *Akedat Yitchak,* he was a fifteenth-century Spanish commentator.

Bechor Shor, Joseph: Twelfth-century French commentator.

HaLevi, Judah: Eleventh-century Spanish philosopher.

Hirsch, Samson Raphael: Eighteenth-century German commentator.

Ibn Ezra, Abraham: Eleventh-century Spanish commentator.

Keli Yakar. Torah commentary written by Solomon Ephraim ben Chaim Lunchitz, a sixteenth-century Polish scholar.

Kimchi, David: Twelfth-century French-Spanish commentator.

Luzzato, Chayim: Eighteenth-century Italian commentator.

Maimonides, Moses: Eleventh-century medieval Jewish philosopher.

Menachem Mendel of Kotzk: Eighteenth-century Hasidic scholar and commentator.

Midrash Rabbah: Collection of aggadic midrashim to the Torah.

Nachmanides: Thirteenth-century Spanish biblical commentator, his real name was Moses ben Nachman (also known as the Ramban).

Philo Judaeus: First-century philosopher whose Greek writings focused mainly on the Torah.

Rashbam (Samuel ben Meir): Eleventh-century French commentator.

Rashi (Solomon ben Isaac): Eleventh-century French commentator.

Sforno, Obadiah: Sixteenth-century Italian commentator.

Tosefta: A supplement to the Mishnah.

Modern Commentators

Adler, Morris: Twentieth-century Conservative rabbinic thinker.

Buber, Martin: Twentieth-century philosopher whose *Moses* is a commentary on the Book of Exodus.

Cassuto, Umberto: Twentieth-century Italian commentator.

Epstein, Baruch. Author of commentary *Torah Temimah.*

Essrog, Seymour. Twentieth-century Conservative rabbi.

Gillman, Neil: Twentieth-century Conservative theologian.

Groner, Irwin. Twentieth-century Conservative rabbi.

Heschel, Abraham Joshua: Twentieth-century philosopher.

Leibowitz, Nechama: Twentieth-century professor of Bible.

Mendenhall, George: Modern Bible commentator.

Orzach, Shalom. A leading educator in the Conservative movement.

Peli, Pinchas: Twentieth-century scholar whose "Torah Today" column appeared in the *Jerusalem Post.*

Plaut, Gunther: Twentieth-century Reform scholar.

Riskin, Shlomo: Orthodox modern rabbinic commentator, whose Bible commentaries appear in Jewish newspapers nationwide.

Sarna, Nachum: Professor emeritus of Bible studies at Brandeis University.

Schneersohn, Menachem. Twentieth-century Lubavitcher Rebbe and scholar.

Steinsaltz, Adin. Contemporary Israeli talmudist and commentator.

Tigay, Jeffrey. Twentieth-century Bible commentator and professor at the University of Pennsylvania.

Books for Further Study

Buber, Martin. *Moses: The Revelation and the Covenant*. New York: Harper and Row Publishers, 1958.

Cassuto, Umberto. *A Commentary on the Book of Exodus*. Jerusalem: Magnes Press, 1951.

Epstein, Baruch Halevi. *The Essential Torah Temimah*. Shraga Silverstein, trans. Jerusalem: Feldheim Publishers, 1989.

Greenberg, Moshe. *Understanding Exodus*. New York: Behrman House, 1969.

Hertz, Joseph. *The Pentateuch and Haftorahs*. London: Soncino Press, 1988.

Hirsch, Samson Raphael, trans. *The Pentateuch*. London: L. Honig and Sons, 1959.

Leibowitz, Nechama. *Studies in Bereshit, Shemot, Vayikra, Bemidbar, Devarim*. (5 volumes) Jerusalem: World Zionist Organization, 1980.

Mendenhall, George E. *The Tenth Generation*. Baltimore and London: Johns Hopkins Press, 1973.

Peli, Pinchas. *Torah Today*. Washington, D.C: B'nai B'rith Books, 1987.

Plaut, Gunther, ed. *The Torah: A Modern Commentary*. New York: Union of American Hebrew Congregations, 1981.

Sarna, Nahum M. *Understanding Genesis*. New York: Schocken Books, 1966.

Silverman, Hillel E. *From Week to Week*. New York: Hartmore House, 1975.

Speiser, E.A. trans. *The Anchor Bible: Genesis*. New York: Doubleday, 1964.

Zornberg, Avivah Gottlieb. *Genesis: The Beginning of Desire*. Philadelphia: Jewish Publication Society, 1995.